How Believing in a Never-Give-Up God
Will Change Your Life

Holding
On to
HOPE

Heather Quintana

Pacific Press®
Publishing Association
Nampa, Idaho | www.pacificpress.com

Cover design: David Berthiaume
Cover design resources: GettyImages.com
Interior design: Aaron Troia

The author assumes full responsibility for the accuracy of all facts and quotations as cited in this book.

Unless otherwise noted, Scripture quotations are from THE HOLY BIBLE, NEW INTERNATIONAL VERSION®. Copyright © 1973, 1978, 1984, 2011 by Biblica, Inc.® Used by permission. All rights reserved worldwide.

Scripture quotations marked ESV are from The Holy Bible, English Standard Version® (ESV®), copyright © 2001 by Crossway, a publishing ministry of Good News Publishers. Used by permission. All rights reserved.

Scripture quotations marked GNT are from Good News Translation® (Today's English Version, Second Edition) Copyright © 1992 American Bible Society. All rights reserved.

Scripture quotations marked KJV are from the King James Version.

Scripture quotations marked TLB are from *The Living Bible*, copyright © 1971 by Tyndale House Foundation. Used by permission of Tyndale House Publishers Inc., Carol Stream, Illinois 60188. All rights reserved.

Scripture quotations marked NABRE are from the New American Bible, revised edition © 2010, 1991, 1986, 1970 Confraternity of Christian Doctrine, Inc., Washington, DC. All Rights Reserved.

Scripture quotations marked NASB are from the New American Standard Bible®, Copyright © 1960, 1971, 1977, 1995, 2020 by The Lockman Foundation. All rights reserved.

Scripture quotations marked NCV are from the New Century Version®. Copyright © 2005 by Thomas Nelson. Used by permission. All rights reserved.

Scripture quotations marked NLT are from the Holy Bible, New Living Translation, copyright © 1996, 2004, 2007, 2013, 2015 by Tyndale House Foundation. Used by permission of Tyndale House Publishers, Inc., Carol Stream, Illinois 60188. All rights reserved.

Scripture quotations marked NLV are from the New Life Version copyright © 1969 and 2003. Used by permission of Barbour Publishing, Inc., Uhrichsville, Ohio, 44683. All rights reserved.

To order additional copies of this book, call toll-free 1-800-765-6955,
or visit AdventistBookCenter.com.

Library of Congress Cataloging-in-Publication Data
Names: Quintana, Heather, 1975- author.
Title: Holding on to hope : how believing in a never-give-up God will change your life / Heather Quintana.
Description: Nampa, Idaho : Pacific Press Publishing Association, [2023] | Includes bibliographical references. | Summary: "Hoping in the never-give-up God provides comfort for the brokenhearted, rest for the weary, and anticipation for a broken world made new"-- Provided by publisher.
Identifiers: LCCN 2023031741 | ISBN 9780816369713 | ISBN 9780816369720 (ebook)
Subjects: LCSH: Hope--Religious aspects--Christianity.
Classification: LCC BV4638 .Q56 2023 | DDC 234/.25--dc23/eng/20230817
LC record available at https://lccn.loc.gov/2023031741

August 2023

Dedication

For anyone who is losing hope.
Keep holding on.

Contents

Introduction

This book is a pep talk. But it was inspired by a doom-and-gloom person who lived thousands of years ago.

Isaiah, who wrote a lot about judgment and punishment, is known as "the prince of prophets," which is kind of the opposite of "prince of pep talks." He had a somber and serious side, but, interestingly, he also wrote some of the most beautiful, encouraging words in Scripture. He started with thirty-nine chapters of bad news (think, "Woe to the wicked!"), but in chapters 40–66, he lights up the world with a message of hope, restoration, and salvation. At the beginning of the book of Isaiah, he's a preacher in the pulpit, shaking his fists, shouting with a booming voice. But in the second half of the book, he's a friend who runs up and embraces us. He grasps us by the shoulders, looks us in the eye, and assures us in the most tender voice, "Get your hopes up! Good things are on the way. You are not going to be disappointed."

One of the encouraging, hope-filled things that Isaiah wrote has become the inspiration for this book. It is a simple sentence, a prophecy about Jesus, that has significance for our lives even now. It is so important that the disciple Matthew included the prophecy in his gospel account. And now, two thousand years after Matthew wrote about it, I'm writing about it too.

The often-overlooked verse sounds cryptic at first, but as we dust it off and look at it closely, we uncover a remarkable message. Here is the prophesy:

> A bruised reed he will not break,
> and a smoldering wick he will not snuff out (Isaiah 42:3).

In this riddle-like passage we find important information about our never-give-up God and why we can live with expectancy and hope.

This text in Isaiah is a pep talk, but it isn't a shallow, frivolous pep talk. This is a prophecy—a *promise*—that can change how you see absolutely everything in your life. No matter what you're facing, this message will infuse even the most hopeless situations with a new sense of potential and possibility. As we explore this verse from Isaiah, you'll begin to see hope where there once was none. And you'll be reminded that God is cheering you on with this simple, timeless message: hold on to hope.

PART I

The Hidden Promise of Hope

CHAPTER 1

Giving Up on Giving Up

*Never give up then, for that's just the place
and time that the tide'll turn.*
—Harriet Beecher Stowe

Giving up is not an option, according to the old motivational saying. But try telling that to the dusty in-line skates in my garage, the violin I played for one semester in college, or my abandoned box of crafting supplies that is now older than a tenth grader. I've given up on plenty of things, and I have a stack of reminders to prove it.

The truth is that giving up *is* an option, and it's often the easiest one. But giving up is rarely the most satisfying option. Quitting often leaves you with a strange mixture of relief and disappointment. You feel relieved because the pressure is off but disappointed because something inside you wanted to do that thing you quit—otherwise, you wouldn't have started it in the first place.

Those of us who know the disappointing relief of giving up have a special appreciation for people who have the grit to keep going. That's why we cry at movies based on true stories of overcomers who never gave up. It's why we cheer when we see someone running forward in life even when they're tired.

Is it crazy to refuse to give up?

Ron Avitzur considered himself lucky. It was the 1990s, and he had been hired by Apple as a contractor on a secret project: creating a graphing calculator.[1] It was a job he loved so much he would have done it for free. In fact, that's what he ended up doing.

Even though the project had a promising start, it became bogged down by ego and bureaucracy and was eventually canceled.[2] Many contractors were transferred to other projects; however, Ron's contract was terminated. But Ron felt like there was unfinished business: he believed strongly that this calculator needed to exist and that it would be an especially important tool for students and educators.[3]

So he kept showing up for work even though he had been fired.

He quietly pulled in others to help him, and he worked on the project between twelve and sixteen hours a day, seven days a week. He didn't quit when the paychecks stopped coming. He didn't quit when his electronic badge was deactivated and he had to rely on others to let him in the building. He didn't quit when Apple employees kept asking who he was and why he was there. He didn't quit when the facilities manager gave his office to someone else. He didn't quit when a computer monitor he was working on randomly burst into flames.[4]

After six months of unpaid labor, working nearly around the clock and refusing to give up, Ron's graphing calculator was ready. He gave a demonstration of it to the directors at Apple—and they loved it. Ron's creation became a part of every Macintosh computer in 1994. In the decades that followed, it was loaded on millions of machines.[5]

Ron has a great story because his never-give-up attitude led to success. But let's be honest: if it hadn't worked out, the story would be that he was a strange man who trespassed and wouldn't go away even after he was fired.

We know the sensible thing for Ron to do would have been to pack his things and leave, but something in our hearts is drawn to the boldness of a hope that never gives up. We all face moments in our lives when it seems crazy to keep holding on to hope. We just can't seem to let go, not yet, not easily. In those moments, we have to decide if we're going to keep hoping even when things seem hopeless.

Maybe you've carried a dream in your heart for years, but now it seems too late for it to come true.

Maybe you have hopes for reconciliation with a friend or family member, but it has been so long since you talked that the distance seems too great.

Maybe you always wanted to try a new job or a new city, but you feel stuck where you are.

Maybe you have goals to get healthier, or lose weight, or stop smoking, but you keep giving up after a few weeks . . . or days . . . or hours.

Maybe you've given up on yourself and are starting to think you simply don't have what it takes.

When met with resistance or rejection, it's tempting to give up. But what if you're giving up too soon?

Throughout this book, as we explore Isaiah's prophecy, we'll find that when Jesus looks at situations others consider hopeless, He sees a world of potential and possibility. Because of His never-give-up spirit, He sees what *could be*, not just what *is*.

This is the promise and the hope: Jesus doesn't give up easily, and He doesn't want us to either.

---

1. Ron Avitzur, "The Graphing Calculator Story," *Pacific Tech*, accessed June 27, 2023, http://www.pacifict.com/Story/.

2. Avitzur.

3. Julia Dahl, "When His Project Was Canceled, an Unemployed Programmer Kept Sneaking Into Apple to Finish the Job," *Mental Floss*, July 2, 2012, https://www.mentalfloss.com/article/31077/when-his-project-was-canceled-unemployed-programmer-kept-sneaking-apple-finish-job?fbclid=IwAR1lLgda3n9weSULvdBN5tAF4os43CBtIBDbDs0we4U0soyiXuvpXzzNF9A.

4. Avitzur, "Graphing Calculator Story."

5. Avitzur.

CHAPTER 2

Expect the Unexpected

*Unexpected results are the rule
rather than the exception.*

—Plautus

When I was in graduate school, I had a highly sociable friend who often told stories about her wide circle of friends and acquaintances, including someone named Q. Over time, after hearing a few stories, I formed an idea in my mind of what each of these friends was probably like.

Meanwhile, I met another student who introduced himself to me as Robert. He was easy to talk to and eventually mentioned that his full name is Robert Quintana.

"But people call me Q," he said casually.

Oh, Robert is Q! I realized. *He's not what I expected.* He was dressed in outdoorsy clothes and hiking boots. With his eager laugh and big smile, he connected almost instantly with people. I had heard stories about him, but this was not how I had pictured him. I had imagined him quieter and more reserved, wearing chinos and a button-up.

Robert wasn't what I expected. He was, in fact, *better*

than I expected. So much better that I married him.

That was not what I expected

Maybe something like this has happened to you too. You heard about someone before you met them, but when you meet them face-to-face, they aren't at all what you expected. Maybe they were more talkative than you imagined, or taller, or kinder, or ruder.

The longer you think about someone or hear about them before meeting them, the more your mind creates expectations of what they will be like. Sometimes we build these expectations unknowingly, without realizing that our minds have started to paint pictures of an individual.

Consider how long people had been waiting for a Messiah when Jesus came to Earth. For centuries, people had been longing for the promised Savior to arrive. And all that time they were imagining what characteristics the Rescuer would have.

Before we look more closely at Isaiah's cryptic prophecy about what Jesus would be like, it's helpful to consider what the people of the day *expected* Him to be. Their expectations, of course, were strongly influenced by the world in which they lived, including their hardships and struggles.

When Jesus arrived on Earth, people were burdened and breaking under the weight of anxiety and worry. The Jewish people were under Roman rule. The political leaders were corrupt and cruel, weighing down the people with heavy taxes and hopeless futures. And should anyone even consider breaking a law, they only had to look to the hills to see an intimidating reminder of the Romans' signature form of punishment: the Romans would nail a lawbreaker to a wooden cross and let them die gasping for breath.

It should come as no surprise, then, that many of the Jewish people imagined that the coming deliverer would need to be an aggressive, bold leader who would overpower the political rulers of the day. He would be an earthly king above other kings who would end the chaos and set things right. Perhaps he would have military power and would bring freedom by the sword.

Meanwhile, the religious system was just as broken as the political system. The priests were more concerned about getting money than giving hope. The synagogue became their business headquarters where they turned a profit and turned from God. After all, they needed a steady stream of revenue to pay for their luxurious lifestyle.

In addition, the religious leaders insisted that the Jews comply with a list of rules so exhaustive and impossible that people's shoulders slumped under the weight. For every commandment given to the ancient Israelites, the Jewish leaders tacked on clarifications and additions. For example, instead of simply instructing people not to work on the Sabbath, the Jewish scholars created thirty-nine categories of work—and each of those categories had subcategories.[1] Each word and idea expanded, until that one commandment literally grew into thousands of rules, including how many steps were allowed on Sabbath[2] or how many letters could be written on Sabbath.[3]

Because religion had become so distorted, some Jews expected the Messiah to arrive as a purehearted religious leader who would defend the people and eliminate religious corruption. Either way—whether the Savior came through the political system or the religious system—people expected Him to be powerful.

As the people's hardships and expectations grew, it seemed that surely the time was right for the Savior to arrive. There was a feeling in the air. Things couldn't go on this way much longer. He must be on His way.

And that's when the scammers and con artists showed up. For years, charismatic men—some charming, some angry—had claimed to be the long-awaited redeemer. Maybe some of the self-proclaimed messiahs believed they actually were the One; maybe some just wanted power or money. Either way, they came with boldness, hoping their fiery overconfidence would convince people to trust them.

The low-key, low-status plan

Through it all, the Jews had expectations. And they were watching the horizon for a larger-than-life, mighty hero to arrive. Eyes squinting against the sun, they searched the highways and hills, the synagogues and the towns, looking for that regal king or holy priest who would set them free.

It never crossed their minds to look in a barn.

People were looking for the deliverer, not the delivery of a baby.

Jesus came at just the right time—in, as Paul said, "the fullness of time" (Galatians 4:4, ESV)—but not the way people expected.

Rather than arriving as an invincible, supernatural warrior, Jesus came as a tiny, fragile baby. When He arrived, He didn't show up shouting against corruption; He couldn't even talk. He wasn't charging toward the dishonest leaders; He couldn't even walk.

He was so small and fragile that when Joseph picked him up, young Mary might have exclaimed, "Careful, don't drop Him!"

We've heard the story so many times that the absolute absurdity is almost lost on us. It has nearly laughable charm. Our best and greatest Hope was drooling, crying, wiggling on a pile of hay in a barn.

The years that followed were equally void of prestige for the child Messiah. Jesus' parents were just regular people. He was raised in Nazareth, a town so appalling and despised that there was a common insult: "Can anything good come out of Nazareth?" (John 1:46, ESV).

And while the eternal future of every single human rested on His shoulders, the carpenter Jesus was in a workshop, whistling, hunched over a saw, bending down to smooth the rough edges of a piece of wood as He built tables and chairs. Instead of stepping back with a grand gesture and taking in the view of the whole earth, He was stepping back from a workbench and looking with satisfaction at a wooden bowl or chair, each an insignificant masterpiece.

---

1. Ronald L. Eisenberg, "Shabbat's Work Prohibition," My Jewish Learning, accessed August 3, 2023, https://www.myjewish learning.com/article/shabbats-work-prohibition/.

2. W. J. Fallis, "Sabbath Day's Journey," in *Holman Bible Dictionary*, ed. Trent C. Butler (Nashville, TN: Holman Bible Publishers, 1991), 1216, 1217.

3. Mendy Wineberg, "Koteiv—Writing," Chabad.org, accessed August 3, 2023, https://www.chabad.org/library/article_cdo/aid /5152314/jewish/Koteiv-Writing.htm.

CHAPTER 3

He's Not What You Expect, but He's What You Need

*God has promised to meet
our needs, not our greeds.*
—Loren Cunningham

Matthew was part of Jesus' inner circle of disciples and friends. He was a Jew, but the truth is that his fellow Jews probably didn't like him very much. Before He met Jesus, he served as a tax collector for Rome, gathering greedy amounts of money from his own family and neighbors. As you might imagine, they weren't happy to see him coming.

But, once Matthew met Jesus, he left his job with the Roman Empire to join Jesus' humble revolution. He was by Jesus' side as He preached, healed, and befriended the forgotten and unloved. And when Jesus was arrested, crucified, resurrected, and returned to heaven—Matthew experienced all of it firsthand.

After living through so many adventures with Jesus, Matthew didn't forget about his fellow Jews, the people from whom he had once taken money. Now he wanted to give something to them, something better than what he had taken. He wanted to give them Jesus. He wanted them to know that Jesus was the Savior of the world, the fulfillment of the prophecies they had heard since childhood.

That's why, when Matthew wrote out the stories of Jesus' life, he also included the very scriptures that the Jewish people trusted. In his writings, he referenced prophecies about the Messiah and illustrated how Jesus fulfilled each of those prophecies.

In a way, Matthew was creating a checklist of prophesied characteristics of the Redeemer, and for each item on the list, he showed how Jesus matched it. That's why, as you read through the book of Matthew, you'll notice that he often tells a story about Jesus and says, "This fulfills the prophecy . . ." and then gives a direct quote from a prophetic passage.

Matthew was well qualified to tell Israelites about Jesus because he knew the traditional Jewish interpretations of the old prophecies. He knew the Jews needed to look closely at the specific predictions and reevaluate them, or they would risk missing something—or Someone—very important.

In the end, Matthew's message to the Jews sounded a little like this: "Jesus is not what you expected, but He is the Messiah. And here's the proof."

The gentle leader

In Matthew 12, you'll find one of those items from the prophecy checklist along with a supporting story about Jesus. It's something you might be tempted to skim—Matthew quoting a prophecy from Isaiah—but this passage is the promise of the never-give-up God. This is the prophecy that tells us why we can hold on to hope. Here we find the description of an unexpected trait of the Messiah, the source of our great hopefulness.

Before Matthew quotes the prophesy, he sets it up by telling this personal story:

One day Matthew and the other disciples were walking through a grainfield with Jesus. As they walked, the hungry disciples casually ran their hands over the heads of grain, broke pieces off, and ate the kernels as they walked with Jesus. Some of the Pharisees saw this and confronted them, accusing them of breaking the law by "harvesting grain on the Sabbath" (verse 2, NLT).

Jesus immediately responded by quoting scriptures about the Sabbath, true mercy, and sacrifice. Then He shocked the listeners with a short sentence that was a big claim: "For the Son of Man is Lord of the Sabbath" (Matthew 12:8). Jesus was asserting that He is both the Son of Man (a representative of the people) and the Lord of the Sabbath (a representative of God).

Jesus' declaration of authority infuriated the Pharisees, who were members of a Jewish sect known for strict observance of the law and superior sanctity, which simply means they were self-righteous. They became more determined than ever to shut Him up and shut Him down.

But Jesus wasn't done for the day. He and His followers left that grainfield and went straight to the synagogue.

There they noticed a man with a deformed hand. For Jesus, this was another opportunity to do good. For the Pharisees, it was another opportunity to trap Jesus.

Before Jesus even approached the man, the Pharisees anticipated what Jesus might do. "Looking for a reason to bring charges against Jesus, they asked him, 'Is it lawful to heal on the Sabbath?' " (Matthew 12:10).

As Lord of the universe, Jesus could have forced the pious leaders out of the synagogue. He could have called down lightning to strike them. He could have deformed *their* hands and then asked if *they* wanted to be healed on Sabbath. But he did not raise His voice. He did not argue.

Jesus simply told a story: He asked them to imagine they had a sheep that fell into a pit on Sabbath. "Wouldn't you want to get it out of there, no matter what day it was?" He asked them (see verse 11).

"How much more valuable is a person than a sheep!" Jesus declared. "Therefore it is lawful to do good on the Sabbath" (Matthew 12:12).

Then Jesus turned His attention back to the man with the deformed hand and miraculously restored him to full health.

In both of these interactions—in the field and in the synagogue—Jesus proved Himself an unlikely combination: He was gentle but strong. He didn't fight, but He didn't back down. He wasn't the showiest guy in the room, but He got the most attention. He didn't argue, but He was no pushover.

Songwriter Michael Card describes Jesus this way: "His gaze was kindness, but His stare was stone."[1]

Jesus' quiet strength was a threat to the religious leaders. It made them nervous, and it made them angry. So that afternoon in the synagogue, as a man celebrated his miraculous healing, the Pharisees turned and left the building. They didn't say another word. They just "went out and plotted how they might kill Jesus" (Matthew 12:14).

A day in the life of Jesus

After being challenged throughout the day, first in the field, and then in the synagogue, Jesus "withdrew from that place," according to Matthew (verse 15). But why wouldn't the long-awaited Messiah stand up for Himself? Why would He withdraw and quietly leave the room? That's not what the Jews expected. They thought this would have been the perfect opportunity for Jesus to exert His power.

As Jesus left, a crowd of people started following Him. He surely longed for some rest and silence. But instead of sending them away, He healed and encouraged them, and—here's an important part of the story—He "warned them not to tell others about him" (Matthew 12:16).

No publicity stunts or attention seeking. No major announcements or declarations. In fact, He did the opposite. Amid an enthusiastic crowd of newly healed believers who longed to cheer and shout, He asked them to enjoy the miracles quietly and privately, without drawing attention to Him. He didn't want them to spread the word that the long-awaited Messiah was among them. Not yet, anyway.

He wasn't shouting out who He was, and He asked them not to tell either.

At this point in the telling of the story, Matthew brings in Isaiah's prophecy of the never-give-up God. As Matthew reflected on the day's activities in the field, in the synagogue, and with the crowds, Matthew saw that Jesus' actions were a fulfillment of that prophecy.

We'll look, first, at the entire prophecy that Matthew included, but then we'll concentrate on one important sentence of the prophecy. Matthew wrote:

> This was to fulfill what was spoken through the prophet Isaiah:
> "Here is my servant whom I have chosen,
>   the one I love, in whom I delight;
> I will put my Spirit on him,
>   and he will proclaim justice to the nations.
> He will not quarrel or cry out;
>   no one will hear his voice in the streets.
> A bruised reed he will not break,
>   and a smoldering wick he will not snuff out,
> till he has brought justice through to victory.
>   In his name the nations will put their hope"
>   (Matthew 12:17–21).

Matthew pointed out that, as was prophesied, Jesus wasn't going to fight or scream in the streets. He would start a revolution, but not in the outsized way that most Jews expected. Jesus would not find His power within the existing government. He wasn't going to lead a takeover of the political system or priesthood. He wouldn't build up an army to conquer the territory. A new way forward would emerge, but it wouldn't be through violent battles or war. The only bloodshed would be His own.

---

1. Michael Card, "His Gaze," (2006).

CHAPTER 4

The Smallest Hope

Hope is the thing with feathers
That perches in the soul,
And sings the tune without the words,
And never stops at all.
—Emily Dickinson

Let's focus now on one sentence buried in Isaiah's prophetic description of the Messiah. This sentence reveals the heart of the prophecy and the heart of Jesus:

A bruised reed he will not break,
    and a smoldering wick he will not snuff out (Matthew 12:20).

It's so riddle-like that it's easy to miss the promise. This is how one paraphrase of the verse says it:

He does not crush the weak,
Or quench the smallest hope (Matthew 12:20, TLB).

To illustrate his point, Isaiah described everyday things that people would think of as damaged or inadequate, including a crushed reed and a dim candle (Isaiah 42:3).

Picture a bruised reed by the water's edge, Isaiah told readers. It's a tall piece of grass that has been trampled, flattened. Maybe an animal stepped on it, or a heavy wind has blown it down. It's not completely broken in half, but it's no longer standing tall and strong. Isaiah is pointing out that if Jesus saw that blade of grass, He wouldn't step on it or crush it. He would look at it and see the potential for it to grow tall and sturdy again.

Isaiah's next example is a smoldering wick—a candle that has almost gone out. It's more smoke than flame. If Jesus saw that, He wouldn't extinguish it. Instead of snuffing it out, He would give it time. He would see the potential for it to blaze brightly again.

Both of these things symbolize situations or people that seem a little more broken than whole, more damaged than perfect. To most bystanders, they look hopeless, too far gone. They would appear to have no potential. But when the Messiah sees them, He doesn't just see what they are—He sees what they can be. He doesn't give up on what others consider hopeless.

The prophecy was given to alert people to watch for an unexpected kind of leader. A leader who would be gentle, patient, and fiercely hopeful.

Can you see the possibilities?

The beautiful thing about Isaiah's prophecy is that it wasn't just meant for people thousands of years ago. It is for us too. It is a reminder that when things seem hopeless, Jesus still sees a spark of hope. When you are about to give up—on a dream, a loved one, a relationship, your health, yourself—Jesus still sees life. Nothing is so trampled down that He can't see it standing strong again. Nothing is so dark that He can't see it shining brightly once more.

Over the years, I have spoken at various spiritual retreats and events. One of the presentations I have given is titled "How to Create a God-Inspired Bucket List." For a couple of hours, I walk participants through some interactive exercises to help them identify what they would like to do or would like to see happen in the upcoming years of their lives.

As you might imagine, some of the first things that people add to their lists are related to travel and adventure, things such as visiting Australia, swimming with dolphins, or taking an RV trip across the United States. But I also encourage them to think about other aspects of life, such as their relationships, health, finances, spirituality, and sense of purpose. For instance, maybe they've always dreamed of going back to college or becoming a teacher. Perhaps they want to develop new habits, like exercising regularly or looking people in the eye more often. Maybe they want to learn new skills, like how to make tamales, how to handle conflict, or how to take better photos.

As we discuss different categories, we pause for participants to write down any bucket-list items that come to mind. While most people leave the seminar with a long list of God-inspired ideas, there is always someone who writes nothing on their list. Nothing. They don't speak up, they don't participate, they don't laugh and dream with the others. At some point in the seminar, that skeptic asks some version of this question: "What if a person doesn't have any dreams or goals for their life?"

I always try to spark curiosity, an appreciation for the charms of life. "Is there not one book you'd like to read?" I ask. "What about a picnic—you don't ever want to go on another picnic in your life? Is there someone who has been kind to you over the years to whom you'd like to send a thank-you card? Think of these as goals you could add to your list," I tell them. Having a life list isn't just about a trip to Paris or going skydiving. It's about living an abundant life.

Sometimes I see a flash of interest when I encourage the skeptic in the room. Other times, I'm met with cold, hard resistance. I see defeat in their eyes. They think they have too much wisdom and gravitas to foolishly pull hopes and dreams out of the sky. But what they're demonstrating doesn't look like wisdom: It looks like cynicism. It looks like they've given up hope.

All of us are constantly faced with situations, both large and small, that can steal our sense of hopefulness. One major crisis or disappointment is enough to empty years' worth of hope from your soul. And the small disappointments? Those aren't harmless either. They can wear you down so gradually that you wake up one day wondering how you ended up feeling so defeated.

Fortunately, it's OK to get your hopes up. In fact, you *should* get your hopes up. As Isaiah's prophecy points out, God is so full of hope that He gazes with joyful anticipation at even crushed grass and dim candles. And He is yearning for you to live with high hopes. Once you believe that, life begins to sparkle with possibility.

CHAPTER 5

Bad Things Get Good, and Good Things Get Better

*Hope smiles from the threshold of the year
to come, whispering, "it will be happier."*
—Alfred, Lord Tennyson

"What was your favorite thing about your trip?"

That's a question I always ask people when they come back from vacation. You might be surprised how often people have to stop and think about it before they answer. Whether it was an amazing trip or a disappointing one, their favorite part of it isn't always the first thing that comes to mind. But once they start talking about the high points, they light up as they remember the special experiences.

Just recently, people have told me about these favorite vacation moments:

- watching a sunrise from the top of a fourteener in Colorado
- taking surf lessons in Hawaii
- eating pasta and gelato in Italy
- riding in an airboat through the Everglades

Of all the favorite vacation moments I have heard people talk about, I've never heard anyone say that their favorite part of a trip was any of the following:

- searching online for a rental car
- spending hours checking for hotels and plane tickets
- submitting a vacation request at work
- deciding what to pack while doing last-minute laundry
- going through security at the airport
- requesting the United States Postal Service to hold their mail while they're out of town
- arranging for a pet sitter or asking someone to water their houseplants

Surprisingly, though, research indicates that your vacation-related happiness is tied a lot more closely to that list of dreaded tasks than the list of highlights. A study found that the greatest boost in happiness actually comes from *planning* a vacation, not being on vacation.[1] Some people may experience a small spike in happiness while they are traveling, but most people's happiness quickly drops back to baseline levels as soon as they return home. A getaway creates no lasting increase in joy. In fact, vacationers returning from their travels are no happier than people who haven't gone on vacation at all. Even with a suntan and a souvenir T-shirt, the travelers come back feeling a little let down because the happy experiences are behind them, and now they have to unpack and catch up on routine tasks and work projects.[2]

However, people who are looking forward to a vacation, who know the bright days are still ahead of them, *those* are the happy people. According to researchers, vacation anticipation boosts happiness for up to eight weeks. That means that as unlikely as it seems, the longest lasting burst of happiness doesn't come from going on the vacation but from thinking about and anticipating it.[3]

The thrill of anticipation

It's a principle that applies not only to vacations but also to life in general: knowing that something good is on the way makes us happy, just as happy as when we are *experiencing* something good. That explains how it's possible to be in a dark, disappointing time in life and still have joy—when you know deep in your bones that something better is coming, anticipation of brighter days can keep you joyful.

Simply put, hope is an optimistic outlook that things are going to be OK. Studies show that hopeful people have significant advantages in life. They have better physical health, stronger relationships, healthier habits, and greater longevity.[4] Hopeful people also experience less depression, less anxiety, lower levels of pain,[5] fewer chronic health problems, reduced risk of cancer,[6] and less chance of heart disease.[7] Amazingly, your overall quality of life is impacted more by your level of hopefulness than your circumstances.

The research all points in the same direction: if you want to be happy and healthy, your life doesn't have to be perfect. You just have to remain hopeful that everything is going to work out in the end.

Brighter days ahead

When Isaiah wrote about the patience and hopefulness of the coming Messiah, he described two scenarios: a flattened piece of grass, and a dimming candle. The two examples seem quite similar—two things that don't look very hopeful. But there's a slight difference worth noting. Both objects are in the middle of a process. The bruised grass has been crushed and trampled. It is not completely ruined, but if the crushing continues, that piece of grass is going to be irreversibly destroyed. The smoldering wick, on the other hand, was lit with the intention of the candle burning brightly. If the process continues in *that* direction, the candle will burn with a bright flame.

For the crushed grass, a bad thing needs to get good.

For the smoldering candle, a good thing needs to get better.

This is the spirit of hope. Hope believes that bad things are going to get good, and good things are going to get better. According to the prophet Isaiah, this is also the spirit of Jesus. Whatever the starting point, He sees a bright future. With Jesus, bad things get good, and good things get better.

Isaiah's prophecy is a call to find the joy in anticipation. Good things are on the way. Jesus looks at trampled grass, dim candles, and seemingly hopeless situations, and He smiles over each one, thrilled with the anticipation of all they will become.

King Solomon, known as the wisest man to ever live, also believed that we should anticipate and expect good things. In Proverbs 4:18, he says that if you put your hope in God, things *will* keep getting better and brighter: "The way of the good person is like the light of dawn, growing brighter and brighter until full daylight" (NCV).

Just as you would joyfully anticipate a vacation, you can anticipate that your future holds plenty of good things and happy surprises. You don't have to buy plane tickets or book a hotel to start feeling the thrill of anticipation. Just watch with hopefulness as God amazes you with a future that is brighter than you ever imagined.

---

1. Jeroen Nawijn et al., "Vacationers Happier, but Most not Happier After a Holiday," *Applied Research in Quality of Life* 5, no. 1 (March 2010): 35–47, https://doi.org/10.1007/s11482-009-9091-9.

2. Tara Parker-Pope, "How Vacations Affect Your Happiness," *New York Times*, February 18, 2010, https://archive.nytimes.com/well.blogs.nytimes.com/2010/02/18/how-vacations-affect-your-happiness/?_r=2.

3. Parker-Pope.

4. Everett Worthington, "How Hope Can Keep You Healthier and Happier," The Conversation, March 18, 2020, https://

theconversation.com/how-hope-can-keep-you-healthier-and-happier
-132507.

5. Andrea Bonior, "The Health Benefits of Hope," *Psychology Today*, March 30, 2021, https://www.psychologytoday.com/us /blog/friendship-20/202103/the-health-benefits-hope.

6. Worthington, "Healthier and Happier."

7. Alexandra Sifferlin, "A Happy, Optimistic Outlook May Protect Your Heart," *Time*, April 18, 2012, https://healthland.time .com/2012/04/18/a-happy-mind-may-mean-a-healthy-heart/.

PART II

Holding On to Hope
in Everyday Life

CHAPTER 6

If He Doesn't Give Up, We Won't Either

Our greatest weakness lies in giving up.
—Thomas Edison

OK, it's established: we follow a God who holds on to hope and doesn't give up. Isaiah prophesied it, Matthew recorded it, and Jesus proved it. And now this never-give-up God is calling out for you to get your hopes up and not give up. What will that look like in your daily life? How does it affect your relationships, your health, your dreams, your work, and your faith? In the next few chapters, we'll look at several common areas of life in which we are tempted to give up. In each area, we'll explore practical ways you can hold on to hope in even the shakiest of situations.

As you glance at the topics covered in the upcoming chapters, you may be tempted to read only the ones that address your greatest concerns. Definitely give those chapters special attention, prayerfully asking God to speak hope to you in those areas. You might also notice some chapters that address topics of less interest to you. I encourage you to read them anyway. While you may not immediately feel interested in health or relationships, for example, you might find the Holy Spirit has a prompting or word of encouragement for you in that area. Perhaps a new idea will come to mind or a long-forgotten goal will return to you as you read.

For those areas where you already have abundant hope, let the following pages be an enthusiastic reminder to continue to live in hope and share hope with others. You may have people in your life who are struggling and need you to hold on to hope on their behalf.

And for those areas in life that seem hopeless—such as a project, goal, or relationship—let God breathe new life into them. He does His greatest work when all hope seems lost.

CHAPTER 7
Don't Give Up on Hopeless Situations

*There will come a time when you believe
everything is finished. That will be the beginning.*
—Louis L'Amour

Curt Degerman wore the same filthy blue jacket
every day for forty years. And every day he had the same
routine: he scavenged through dumpsters for his food
and collected metal, mostly tin cans, to sell for pennies
at a recycling plant. The people of Skelleftea, Sweden,
thought of him as their town's harmless oddball. They
even gave him the nickname of Tin-Can-Curt.[1]

Little did they know that when Curt wasn't digging
through trash cans, he was at the public library study-
ing the stock market. He had a sharp mind for finances,
even though he had dropped out of school early in life.
Penny by penny, dollar by dollar, Curt began investing
his meager recycling earnings.[2]

When he died of a heart attack at the age of sixty,
Curt was still eating out of trash cans and picking up
soda cans. But he wasn't penniless, as the community
had assumed. Tin-Can-Curt died a millionaire. He had
a secret fortune in stocks, gold bars, and savings. He

43

had even drafted a will, leaving his estate to a cousin who came to visit him in the months leading up to his death.[3]

It looked like Tin-Can-Curt had nothing except a pocketful of loose change and the dirty jacket on his back, but the town eccentric had a seven-figure net worth.[4]

Curt probably could have taught us a thing or two about investing; but more importantly, he can teach us a lesson about life: things aren't always what they seem. You cannot judge a situation by appearances. Something that looks hopeless to you isn't hopeless to God.

When we face frustrations or difficulties, we may not see a way forward, but God does. The God who hasn't given up on trampled grass and dim candles sees potential and possibility everywhere.

Nothing is impossible for God

Let me assure you of this: God specializes in hopeless situations. He doesn't just endure them or offer up mediocre, this-will-have-to-do outcomes. He takes the impossible and makes something breathtakingly beautiful out of it. He sees you, and He knows right now the exact burden you are quietly carrying. He sees what keeps you up at night, what leaves you feeling hollow or defeated, what makes you fearful or angry. He sees what your situation is now, but more importantly, He sees what it can be. When He looks at a trampled piece of grass, He sees it growing tall again, strong and verdant. When He looks at a dimming candle, He sees it once again bursting into a dazzling flame.

If you don't believe me, open the Bible. Turn to any book of the Bible, and you will find a story or a promise about God turning around a deeply hopeless situation. That's what He does.

- When the Israelites were in slavery, it seemed hopeless.
- When Joseph was in prison, it seemed hopeless.
- When Daniel was thrown into a den of hungry lions, it seemed hopeless.
- When Sarah was almost ninety years old and still wasn't pregnant with the promised baby, it seemed hopeless.
- When young David fought against a raging giant, it seemed hopeless.
- When Shadrach, Meshach, and Abednego were forced into a fiery furnace, it seemed hopeless.
- When Jonah was in the belly of a fish, it seemed hopeless.
- When no doctor could heal the blind, the deaf, the leprous, and the crippled, it seemed hopeless.
- When five thousand men plus their wives and children were famished and the only person who had food was one little boy, it seemed hopeless.

- When Lazarus was dead, it seemed hopeless.
- When Paul was shipwrecked three times, lashed five times, beaten with rods three times, stoned once, alone in the open sea for a night and day, endangered by bandits, and imprisoned more times than he could count, it seemed hopeless.

But none of these situations were hopeless to God. Whatever you are going through, it is not too hopeless for God.

Impossible is God's starting point

Throughout Scripture, we see that great stories often start with hopeless situations. Impossible isn't an ending point for God—it's a starting point. Consider these verses that celebrate the God of the impossible:

- "Jesus looked at them and said, 'With man this is impossible, but with God all things are possible' " (Matthew 19:26).
- "For nothing will be impossible with God" (Luke 1:37, ESV).
- "Is anything too hard for the Lord?" (Genesis 18:14).
- "I know that you can do all things" (Job 42:2).
- "Ah, Lord God! It is you who have made the heavens and the earth by your great power and by your outstretched arm! Nothing is too hard for you" (Jeremiah 32:17, ESV).

After reading what God is capable of doing, we can't help but agree with Paul, who wrote, "What then shall we say to these things? If God is for us, who can be against us?" (Romans 8:31, ESV).

When things seem impossible, that's when God does His best work. When we ask for God's help, it might involve waiting (God has His own timeline, after all) and it might involve surprises (He has ways we can't imagine). But no matter what happens, once the hopeless is handed over to God, we can watch in wonder, knowing that He is the great and endless source of help and hope.

This is the healing crisis

I was in my early thirties when I started losing my energy and feeling a little "off." At first, I just thought I was sleep deprived, maybe a little stressed. But after the fatigue came the aching muscles and burning joints. I dismissed those too, thinking maybe I had exercised too much (or maybe not enough). When the night sweats started, I assumed I had set the thermostat too warm. When my hands and feet began tingling, I thought I must have been sitting too long and my limbs were just falling sleep. But then the seizures came, and I couldn't explain that away. I knew something was definitely wrong.

I wasn't the only one confused by my mysterious symptoms. Over the course of two years, I went from specialist to specialist—until the doctors didn't know where else to send me. When I would have frightening seizures in the middle of the night, my husband would take me to the ER. Finally, one physician told him, "There's no need to keep bringing her back. There's nothing we can do to help."

I was doing everything I could to promote health—eating nutritiously, exercising, prioritizing rest, getting fresh air and sunshine—yet I wasn't getting better.

Finally, a physician assistant in my primary-care doctor's office was flipping through my thick folder of medical records and casually asked, without even making eye contact, "Has anyone ever checked you for Lyme disease?"

No, they had not, I answered.

She ordered a test, and a few days later it was confirmed that I did have Lyme disease, which I had contracted from a tick bite several years earlier. The symptoms were escalating, becoming more complicated and intense, because the condition had gone untreated for so long.

Had the Lyme disease been caught immediately, a month of antibiotics would likely have been the treatment plan; but in this case, a month of pills didn't even begin to chip away at the problems. So we advanced to an antibiotic cocktail, a combination of multiple antibiotics. Still no progress. Eventually, a leading Lyme specialist oversaw a plan for me to receive IV antibiotics at home with the help of a home-health nurse.

But after I began the IVs, I started feeling worse. Worn down, I complained to the doctor that not only was I *not* getting better but that I felt worse than ever before.

"Excellent," he replied.

As he said that, I felt tears coming to my eyes. I didn't see anything *excellent* about this. But he saw things differently than I did.

"This," he continued gently, "is the healing crisis. This is when things get worse before they get better."

He explained that my reaction was perfectly normal. It was not unusual to see a temporary worsening of symptoms when certain bacterial infections, including Lyme disease, are treated with antibiotics. When the Lyme spirochetes, the menacing spiral-shaped bacteria, are being killed off by antibiotics, it can briefly create inflammation that increases the occurrence of fever, headaches, muscle and joint pain, cognitive impairment, and other symptoms.

This crisis was going to make me better, he said.

And it did.

That was a turning point in my recovery from Lyme disease.

Sometimes it feels like you're going through something that is going to crush you. Sometimes you've had a setback or have struggled with something for years, and you feel worse than ever. Sometimes you don't know what else to do because you've tried it all.

Perhaps that is your healing crisis.

You may think things are getting worse, but the Great Physician may be looking at you, saying, "This is excellent. This struggle can help you heal."

God doesn't give up, and He doesn't waste a crisis.

He promises to use even difficult things to bring you greater hope and wholeness. As Paul wrote, "God causes all things to work together for good to those who love God" (Romans 8:28, NASB).

You may be wondering, *But how do I know if I'm having a healing crisis or just a crisis?* If it's a healing crisis, you'll be better at the end of it. And, amazingly, God can somehow turn every crisis into a healing crisis.

Time doesn't heal, but time with God does

A few years ago, my husband and I climbed down a volcano chimney. On the remote island of Terceira, in the middle of the Atlantic Ocean, there's a mountain you can descend into, where lava once came up.

You might expect a volcano to look scorched inside—blackened, dim, and lifeless. But enough time has passed that this cave is now bursting with new life. Every wall is covered with lush greenery. Sunshine streams through the hole where hot lava once tore open the peak of the mountain. And below, a crystal-clear lake sparkles with the rainwater that the mountain has quietly collected since it was ripped open and exposed to the sky.

Standing inside that volcano, I was reminded that something can explode and appear to be destroyed but in the end still become beautiful. A heap of ruins can turn into a place of beauty.

When something in your life feels like it's erupting—a relationship, a job, your finances, your health, your expectations—whatever it is, hold on to hope.

Not all is lost. In the place of loss and destruction, new life can grow again. Beauty can rise up. Light can break through the cracks. It may not look the same as before, but it might end up even better than before.

If you've ever carried a burden or struggle for a long time, you know that time *doesn't* heal all wounds, despite what the old cliché says. If you stubbornly hold on to a grudge or resentment, it continues to burn inside you. Time alone can't heal all wounds, but God can. When we live in surrender and expectancy, trusting God to bring beauty out of disaster, He will.

In addition to reminding us that God doesn't give up easily, Isaiah also wrote that God does holy exchanges: He takes a bad thing and gives a good one in its place. In Isaiah 61:3, there is a promise for those who are discouraged—the Lord will give "beauty for ashes, the oil of joy for mourning, the garment of praise for the spirit of heaviness" (KJV).

So stand tall on your mountain, even if lava flows all around you. There's no need to lose hope. Just give it to God, and then give Him time. The never-give-up God is about to turn your ashes into something beautiful—that's a promise.

When you feel stuck in life

Major disasters and devastating losses are not the only kind of hopeless situations we can face. Sometimes hopeless situations are more subtle, and they come on you slowly. The hopelessness creeps in during mundane days that aren't exactly bad but aren't exactly good either. Life just didn't turn out the way you expected. You thought by now your life would be different. You feel stuck, and you're losing hope that things will ever change or get better.

These are the hopeless situations we usually lock inside and carry alone. When faced with other types of difficulty—like a major health crisis or the loss of a loved one—we might talk to a friend or ask for prayer, but the quiet ache of a disappointing life is not something we bring up at dinner parties. It's not exactly an upbeat conversation starter: "Hi, nice to meet you. I feel like my life is headed nowhere. I am stuck in a dead-end life."

I recently read a news article about two people who were trapped for two days in a janitor's closet in Daytona Beach, Florida. Correction—the couple *thought* they were trapped in a janitor's closet for two days.[5]

When they were finally rescued, the police investigated the area and found that the closet door wasn't locked. It could have been opened anytime. For two long days, they suffered in a small, stuffy area with no food, no water, no bathroom, and no bed, because they were certain they were stuck, even though they weren't.[6]

If you're feeling stuck in life, maybe it's time to try the doorknob. You might not be as stuck as you think you are. Sometimes you can get self-limiting ideas in your mind, and you repeat them until you really do feel trapped: *This is never going to get better. I'll never get ahead. No one will ever love me. I gave up on my dreams a long time ago. This is just the way it is.*

Sometimes the first step in getting unstuck is to stop *thinking* you're stuck. You might be in a difficult place *for now*, but that doesn't mean you'll be there *forever*. As long as you're experiencing any forward motion, you're not stuck. If you're not sure what steps to take, turn off any distractions and ask yourself, *What can I do today that will help me get unstuck?* You'll probably be surprised how quickly answers come to you. *Make the phone call. Check for a new job. Text a friend.* Once you take action, you won't feel quite as stuck.

The Bible makes it clear that God longs to take you to new places and teach you new things. In Isaiah, we're given this reminder that God doesn't want you to get stuck in old, lifeless ways:

> See, I am doing a new thing!
>   Now it springs up; do you not perceive it?
> I am making a way in the wilderness
>   and streams in the wasteland (Isaiah 43:19).

God wants to do new things in your life, and He asks, "Do you perceive it? Do you see it?"

If you don't see those areas where He is trying to get you unstuck, pray to see the new things He is doing. And pray for the courage to joyfully follow Him into those new things. Once you have an idea of how to get unstuck, reach for the doorknob, open the door, and go for it. You might not be as stuck as you thought.

Life gets five out of five stars

Research shows that approximately nine out of ten people read online reviews. Whether they are making a purchase, planning a trip, or choosing a business, people not only check online reviews—they trust them. Nearly eighty-five percent of people trust online reviews as much as they would trust a friend's recommendations.[7]

Relying so heavily on online reviews is tricky, though, because consumers are more likely to focus on the negative than the positive. In fact, studies show that people are much more likely to write a bad review than a good one.[8] While a satisfied customer goes merrily about their day, a disappointed one takes the time to type out their frustrating experience.

Take, for instance, these actual online reviews of beloved locations. Regarding the Grand Canyon, one reviewer said it left him bored and expecting more. It was just "a hole. A very, very large hole."[9] When describing Yellowstone National Park, one reviewer advised potential visitors not to waste their time on the geysers, hot springs, and hydrothermal wonders, saying, "Save yourself some money. Boil some water at home."[10] Tumon Beach in Guam received only three out of five stars from one online reviewer because the "beach is too sandy."[11] Meanwhile, another traveler gave the Great Wall of China a bad review, calling it "just a wall."[12]

If you look at life through the eyes of a critic, you will always find something negative, no matter where you are or what you're experiencing. Fortunately, the opposite is true too: if you look at life through lenses of gratitude, you will be able to see something good, even in the hardest of times.

Sometimes you have to ask yourself if you're so caught up in hopelessness that you're missing glimmers of hope.

I'm not asking you to deny the fact that something terrible has happened or that things aren't going the way you would like.

I'm not asking you to accept toxic positivity and chant "I'm fine! It's fine! *Everything is fine!*" while things burn down all around you.

Instead, I'm asking you to put God's Word to the test. He promises that if you give life a good review, He will give you peace. And in the end, peace feels a lot like hope.

The apostle Paul explains that the path to peace begins by looking around and noticing *anything* good in a situation:

Finally, brothers and sisters, whatever is true, whatever is noble, whatever is right, whatever is pure, whatever is lovely, whatever is admirable— if anything is excellent or praiseworthy—think about such things. Whatever you have learned or received or heard from me, or seen in me—put it into practice. And the God of peace will be with you (Philippians 4:8, 9).

Now, I wouldn't take this advice from someone who had never faced hardships and hopeless situations. But Paul? I'll hear him out on this because he had some dark days. In fact, he was writing this piece of advice while in prison. Talk about an excuse to give a place a bad review. Paul's review could have been, "This prison is filthy, stinky, and dark. I'm lonely, shackled, and starving. There's no bathroom. I am trapped! Zero stars. Do not recommend."

Instead Paul took his own advice. "I have learned to be content whatever the circumstances," he wrote in that letter from prison (Philippians 4:11). In other words, when Paul set his mind to it, he could even give prison a decent review: "This prison cell is bigger than the last one I had. I have plenty of time to write letters to churches, and I have the privacy to pray whenever I want. Three out of five stars!"

Even in the most difficult times—*especially* in the difficult times—keep your eyes open for the good, for any glimpse of hope from God. One way to do this is to practice the gratitude exercise known as Three Good Things. Each night before going to bed, think of three good things that happened during the day, and write them down. Humans naturally tend to remember negative events more easily than positive ones (a tendency referred to as negativity bias), but this simple practice can help retrain your brain and "counteract the negativity bias."[13] Recording three good things every day "can give us a sense of purpose and meaning, recharge our energy, and improve our relationships." Additionally, this practice of gratitude can lead to increased life satisfaction, decreased depression, and lower levels of burnout.[14]

The importance of gratitude is astonishing, but it shouldn't really surprise us. Gratitude is a form of praise, after all. And the Bible repeatedly reminds us how important it is to come before God with praise and thanksgiving. As David wrote, "Praise the Lord. Give thanks to the Lord, for he is good; his love endures forever" (Psalm 106:1).

Is this hopelessness or uncertainty?

When you are in the middle of disappointing or difficult circumstances and you have no idea how or when they are going to end, hopelessness sneaks in. If you were certain this trial was only temporary and that it was going to have a happy ending, it would be easier to endure. It's the uncertainty that can leave you flattened with fear, dread, and discouragement.

But don't confuse uncertainty with hopelessness. Things can be uncertain but still hold potential and positivity. In fact, when you aren't sure how things are going to turn out, that is the very time to hold on to hope. As you do what is possible, including looking for the best in dreary situations, you can leave the seemingly impossible with God. You'll be amazed by the peace that comes when you hand things over to the never-give-up God.

Holding On to Hope

1. Anny Shaw, "Secret Millionaire: Tin-Can-Curt, the Tramp Who Made £1m From Recycling Cans," *Daily Mail*, March 31, 2010, https://www.dailymail.co.uk/news/article-1262496/Secret-millionaire-Relatives-tramp-1m-recycling-old-tin-cans-settle-inheritance-feud.html.

2. Shaw.

3. Shaw.

4. Shaw.

5. Andres Jauregui, "Florida Couple Spent Days in Unlocked Closet, Thought They Were Trapped: Cops," *HuffPost*, January 2, 2015, https://www.huffpost.com/entry/florida-couple-trapped-closet-john-arwood-amber-campbell_n_6406464.

6. Jauregui.

7. Craig Bloem, "84 Percent of People Trust Online Reviews as Much as Friends. Here's How to Manage What They See," *Inc.*, July 31, 2017, https://www.inc.com/craig-bloem/84-percent-of-people-trust-online-reviews-as-much-.html.

8. Justine Lubag, "Why People Are More Likely to Leave a Negative Review Than a Positive Review," Rize Reviews News, Rize Reviews, February 2, 2023, https://rizereviews.com/why-people-are-more-likely-to-leave-a-negative-review-than-a-positive-review/.

9. Amber Share, *Subpar Parks: America's Most Extraordinary National Parks and Their Least Impressed Visitors* (New York: Plume, 2021), 95.

10. Share, 114.

11. David Landsel, "15 of the Most Hilarious (and Insane) Trip Advisor Reviews of All Time, Ever," Airfarewatchdog, July 16, 2015, https://www.airfarewatchdog.com/blog/24343464/15-of-the-most-hilarious-and-insane-tripadvisor-reviews-of-all-time-ever/.

12. Landsel.

13. Trinh Mai, Jean Whitlock, and Rob Davies, "How to Practice Three Good Things," Accelerate Learning Community, April 23, 2021, https://accelerate.uofuhealth.utah.edu/explore/how-to-practice-three-good-things.

14. Mai, Whitlock, and Davies.

CHAPTER 8

Don't Give Up on Your Dreams

*The greater danger for most of us lies not
in setting our aim too high and falling short;
but in setting our aim too low,
and achieving our mark.*

—Michelangelo

What would you do if you had $150 million?

For award-winning actor Nicolas Cage, that wasn't a hypothetical question. As a top earner in Hollywood, Cage had a net worth once estimated at $150 million.[1] With that kind of money, a person could spend $20,000 every day for twenty years and still have millions in the bank. It seems like more than enough for one lifetime, but Cage lost the entire fortune in just a matter of years.

Financial news reports show that Cage blew through much of his money buying oddities and eccentric items, including the first comic book to feature Superman, dinosaur skulls, shrunken Pygmy heads, an octopus, a crocodile, albino cobras, a house thought to be haunted, two private islands, and two European castles.[2]

His lavish spending eventually caught up with him—and he lost most of his millions. While he sold most of his resources to pay his debts,[3] some of it he couldn't sell. For example, one of the dinosaur skulls, valued at hundreds of thousands of dollars, had to be returned to the Mongolian government because it had been obtained illegally.[4]

Most of us will never have $150 million, so we can't be entirely sure how we would spend it. But we all have something else incredibly valuable—priceless, really. We have resources, including talents, skills, ambition, and time. And the truth is we waste a lot of it on worthless junk.

Instead of starting that business we always dreamed of, we binge-watch TV. Instead of doing an art project or going on a bike ride, we mindlessly scroll through social media. We argue about politics and watch cat videos and numb ourselves with food or alcohol. We have a fortune inside us, and we waste it on things no more valuable than a comic book, an octopus, or a haunted house.

Some dreams die, others live on

Most of us will give up on a few things before our lives are over, whether it's a job, a relationship, a hobby, or a diet. But when it comes to things we give up, it seems like dreams are often the first to go. When we're young, dreaming is easy and encouraged. If an adult asks a child what they want to be when they grow up and the child replies with something ambitious—"An astronaut!" "A scientist who cures cancer!" "The president of the United States!"—the adult smiles, nods, or chuckles with delight. "You can be anything you want," adults tell children, as we cheer on the tiny people who don't even know how to spell their own names yet.

But somewhere along the way, we add fine print to the claim that you can be anything you want. Well, you can be anything you want except *that* . . . or *that* . . . or, well, *that* is probably too ambitious for you as well. And you don't have the money or influence or connections to do *that other thing* either, so go ahead and mark that off your list too.

Oh, how the heart withers and shrinks when dreams, one by one, get left behind. Something inside us dies.

Of course, there are some dreams we grow out of. When you were five, you might have wanted to be an astronaut, but as you got older you realized that rockets probably aren't for you, especially considering you get motion sickness sitting in the back seat of a car. Or maybe as a child you wanted to be a pirate because you liked the idea of living on a ship and having a parrot on your shoulder. But as an adult you realized that piracy doesn't offer health insurance or a 401(k)—and as far as pets go, you'd rather have a kitten than a wild, exotic bird. Not to mention that pirates aren't exactly friendly, so they usually don't get invited to parties.

So it is that sometimes we give up certain dreams for better dreams. We give up ideas we love for ideas we love more. We realize what kind of plans and ideas are a better fit for us, or we're awakened to dreams bigger than what we previously imagined.

At one point in your life, there was probably something you wanted—desperately wanted. A specific job, house, relationship, or opportunity: you would have given almost anything to make it work. But looking back now? Well, *now* you're glad it didn't happen.

In those cases, even though you wished and begged and prayed for one thing, you ended up with something else, something better. Thankfully.

But there are other dreams—the *God-given* dreams—that feel like they are a part of who you are, just like your height or your eye color. No matter how old you get, no matter who says they can't be attained, you still carry these dreams in your heart. You might not talk about these dreams anymore, because the more time that passes, the more impossible they seem. But these God-inspired dreams are the ones you must not give up on. They might seem like a trampled blade of grass or a dim candle, but God looks at them and still sees life and light. God hasn't given up on them, and you shouldn't either.

Do you want the good news or the bad news?

What about the dream you just can't shake? I've got good news, and I've got bad news.

The good news is there's still hope.

The bad news is it's going to take some work.

That's not *bad* news, exactly, but it's discouraging for

some. Many people want to achieve the dream without having to clock in. It doesn't feel especially glamorous to have a to-do list, a spreadsheet, or a budget. To approach each day with structure and self-discipline isn't always exciting. But these are the ordinary tools that get us extraordinary results. Fortunately, chipping away at a goal doesn't have to be total drudgery. It can feel satisfying and rewarding.

Perhaps there have been times when you heard a song, and it filled you with a burst of hopefulness about your dreams. Maybe a podcast or inspirational speaker got you pumped about your goals. Maybe you read an encouraging quote and thought, *Yes, I absolutely can do this! I can accomplish what God has placed in my heart.*

Those moments bring a spike of emotion that feel like a fresh start, a second wind, a wave of enthusiasm. It's like the feeling you get when you flip the calendar to January. *New Year, new you! Anything is possible!* But dreams, just like New Year's resolutions, are often abandoned and forgotten before they have a fighting chance. One study found that most people give up on their New Year's resolution less than a month after they start.[5] That means on January 1, it's "new year, new you," but by February 1, it's "new year, old you."

After you have a spike of hopefulness about achieving a dream or goal, it's common to have a drop-off of enthusiasm. That first day, you might say you're going to exercise every day or work on your new business idea every evening, but then you get busy or tired and you don't see progress happening quickly enough. And, before you know it, the dream that you hoped would become a reality fades back to exactly that—a dream.

What is stopping you from achieving your dream?

If you carry the disappointment of abandoned dreams, you're not alone. One survey found that only 4 percent of people feel they are living up to their full potential.[6] That means 96 percent of us know that we have untapped potential.

Of course, you, like everyone else, surely have a reason why you gave up on your dream. It must be a pretty good reason; otherwise, you wouldn't have convinced yourself to quit. The problem is that sometimes you believe the things you tell yourself, even when they aren't true. Plenty of us settle for a smaller life than what God wants for us because of the lies we hold on to.

Consider some of these common reasons people give up on their dreams. Maybe you've used one of these excuses yourself:

- *Excuse 1: "There are too many 'toos.'"*

    It's too late. It's too big. It takes too much time. It takes too much work. It takes too much money.

    If you can't see how every part of your dream is going to come together, that doesn't mean the dream should die. It just means you can't see into the future. Fortunately, God can. And if you have placed your life and dreams in His hands, He'll take care of things—past, present, and future.

God doesn't collect every upcoming detail of your life and run it by you for approval first. He's not a secretary who puts all the information in a folder and places it on your desk for approval and a signature. If He showed you all the obstacles and challenges you'll face as you pursue your dream, you might be tempted to quit and stay exactly where you are.

But not to worry. No matter how many "toos" you have associated with your dream, know that it's not too much for Him. He loves when we, the beautiful creations He dreamed up, become fully alive and reflect His image by dreaming up dreams and creating beauty too.

- ***Excuse 2: "Other people are already doing it better than I could."***

  On a warm day in the 1800s, philosopher and economist Vilfredo Pareto stood in the middle of his garden in Italy. The story is told that he noticed 20 percent of his pea plants seemed to be generating 80 percent of the peas. It was a simple idea, but it led him to develop what is now known as the Pareto principle, or the 80/20 rule, which states that "80% of results will come from just 20% of the action."[7] Pareto went on to investigate multiple industries and found that the principle applies across the board.[8]

This garden insight has stood the test of time, with industries still reporting its truth. In various analyses, it has been suggested that "20% of the sales reps generate 80% of total sales," while "20% of customers account for 80% of total profits."[9] In other fields, "20% of [medical] patients account for 80% of health-care spending," while "20% of software bugs cause 80% of software crashes."[10]

If you've been involved in church life, you've probably heard some version of the 80/20 rule there too: "A mere 20 percent of church volunteers do 80 percent of the work." Ask any pastor or church leader, and they will tell you that they'd love to have more volunteers. They want more than 20 percent of congregants to contribute.

But one of the most common excuses people give for not getting involved sounds something like this: "Other people can do that better than I can. Ask *them* to do it." Instead of thinking of what they can offer, many individuals think first of what *other* people can offer. Someone else can sing better, cook better, or teach better. As they focus on what others have to offer, they often overlook the unique contribution they could bring.

Author and clergyman Henry Van Dyke made this observation: "Use what talents you possess: the woods would be very silent if no birds sang there except those that sang best."[11]

It's a big world with a lot of people in it, so someone else is probably already doing some version of your dream. But because it's a big world with a lot of people in it, we need more than one person doing that thing. Why should only one bird sing in the woods? Or only one dolphin leap in the ocean? Or only one person write a book? Or only one person start a business?

God placed specific gifts, interests, and dreams inside you to be used at this very time and place. You have a unique personality and perspective, and you can make a difference that others can't.

According to 1 Peter 4:10, "Each of you should use whatever gift you have received to serve others." You'll notice that there is no fine print that states, "Exceptions apply. If you can name someone who has the same gift and they are better at it than you are, you do not have to use your gift." No, you were given a gift and God encourages you to use it and see what brave, beautiful things happen as a result.

- *Excuse 3: "I don't know if this is God's idea or mine."*

  When you take time to become quiet and contemplative, you may question if your dreams are something God wants or if they're just something *you* want. To answer that, start by asking yourself this question: "Am I seeking this dream so I can get approval, attention, wealth, revenge, or a sense of self-worth?"

  If your answer is yes, you're probably being fueled by self-focused motives that will leave you feeling like you've lost more than you gained, no matter the outcome. Fortunately, even if your dreams are weighed down with striving and selfishness, you are not in an unredeemable situation. Pray and surrender your dreams to God. Hand them over to Him to do with as He sees best. Maybe His dream for you is buried under the one you came up with, or maybe He has a different dream for you, an even better one than you imagined.

  Even when dreams seem entirely unselfish and altruistic, they can drift into something self-centered if they aren't continually surrendered to God. Here is the key to dreams: hold on, but hold on loosely. Doing so allows God to modify and stretch and grow your dreams—and you.

  There is a simple, six-word prayer that can

keep all your dreams focused and faithful. With each step you take toward your dreams, say this prayer: "May it be to Your glory." Six little words. That is a prayer He will never say no to.

Jesus Himself expressed that same sentiment: "Let your light shine before others, that they may see your good deeds and glorify your Father in heaven" (Matthew 5:16). In other words, shine brightly in the world, and let God get all the glory.

Paul gave similar counsel: "So whether you eat or drink or whatever you do, do it all for the glory of God" (1 Corinthians 10:31). Whatever your dreams or goals, approach every endeavor with the intention that you want God to get the glory, not you.

- **_Excuse 4: "I can't do it."_**

  Oddly, the fact that a dream seems too big to do on your own might be a good indicator that the dream is from God. It only makes sense that He inspires you to do things that require you to rely on Him. If you could do it on your own, you probably would—which means you might forget to include Him. But if the dream simply isn't doable without Him, then He gets to share it with you and He gets the glory.

  If you are held back by doubts, know that you are in good company. Spiritual giants like

Moses, Gideon, and Jeremiah all tried the "I can't do it" excuse with God, and He didn't let any of them off the hook. Instead, He promised to be with them if they stepped out in faith. He's telling you the same thing.

He's telling you what He told Moses when he made excuses: "I will be with you" (Exodus 3:12).

He's telling you what He told Gideon when he made excuses: "I will be with you" (Judges 6:16).

He's telling you what He told Jeremiah when he made excuses: "I am with you" (Jeremiah 1:8).

In the end, I'm sure these men were glad God didn't accept their excuses. If they had let their excuses hold them back, they never would have experienced the thrill of God showing up and helping them do something eternally significant.

- *Excuse 5: "I tried and it didn't work."*

Babies are cute. So are kittens. And puppies too. This isn't just my opinion. Research supports these statements. In a study about cuteness, researchers found that people think of young things—such as babies, kittens, and puppies— as the cutest things in the world. According to the research, the sight of a baby human or a baby animal awakens joy in our brains—and it makes us feel affection and compassion toward them. The cuteness triggers our nurturing instinct, which is associated with caregiving and bonding.[12]

Interestingly, we like cute babies even though they are messy and don't know how to do much of anything. They can't hold a spoon or walk across the room. They can't say their name or change their own clothes. But we know they will eventually learn. They just need some time and practice. In fact, the newness and innocence of their wobbly attempts make them *even cuter*. We ooh and aah and clap at their roly-poly attempts to walk, and we laugh and delight in their squishy faces covered with food that didn't make it into their mouths.

Even though we give babies plenty of time and patience to master life skills, we don't go so easy on ourselves. When we, as adults, try something new, we think everything needs to come together quickly. We want to look like we know what we're doing. We don't want to experience failure. When we attempt something but aren't immediately perfect at the task, we don't think it's cute, like a wobbly kitten trying to walk or a cooing baby trying to talk. We think we should give up because clearly we must not be good at this.

But what if, when God sees our messy, wobbly attempts, it awakens in Him affection and compassion, just like it does when we see cute little things? Just like our nurturing instinct is triggered when we see a little baby trying a new task, what if our attempts trigger God's nurturing instinct for us, and our attempts make Him even more excited to help us?

Sometimes we take ourselves too seriously when we're trying new things. Maybe God wants us to have the joy of a baby or a puppy—finding delight and laughter in the trying. Maybe He applauds our shaky steps, just like we clap and cheer for an unsteady baby who plops down on their diapered bottom after taking just a few steps. Maybe He oohs and aahs just like we would do when we watch a video of a fumbling kitten or a shaky baby elephant trying to walk. (Really, watch a video of a baby elephant trying to walk. It will make your day.)

Things worth doing are rarely mastered on the first try. It takes practice and multiple attempts. If you have tried going after a dream or goal but have given up, here are some questions to ask yourself:

○ *Am I quitting too soon?*

In our fast-paced world, we're used to being able to get things almost instantly, so it's easy to develop unrealistic expectations of how soon we'll see results on a goal. If we work out for a week and don't see bulging biceps by the end of the week, we give up. But you may not need to give up—you may just need more practice, information, or time.

○ *What can I do differently next time to change the outcome?*

When things don't go as planned, it can immediately bring on a rush of emotion, whether it's anger, embarrassment, disappointment, or sadness. After some time has passed, try to look back on your attempts through the lens of your *thoughts*, not just your *feelings*. When you think about the failure now, were there some things you could have done differently, such as prepare more or ask for help? Your results might be completely different next time if you find a mentor or create a step-by-step plan in advance.

○ *Did I have realistic expectations?*

Let's say that you did your first public speaking engagement, and your voice sounded a little shaky or you lost your train of thought. Maybe you left the stage thinking, *That was terrible. I'm never doing that again!* You must remember: you're a beginner. You can't compare yourself to someone who has been a public speaker for decades. If on that first attempt you didn't sound like an expert, that's fine—because you *weren't* an expert. You were a beginner. Everyone was a beginner once. It takes time to become the person you will be, so don't let unrealistic expectations cause you to give up.

Excuses, excuses

I recently read a roundup of excuses that real people gave their employers for why they couldn't come in to work that day. Here are a few of them:

- "I got my arm stuck in the blood pressure machine at the grocery store, and I couldn't get it out."
- "I put my uniform in the microwave to dry, and it caught on fire."
- "My false teeth flew out the window while I was driving down the highway."
- "Someone glued my doors and windows shut, so I can't leave my house."
- "I ate cat food instead of tuna, and now I'm deathly ill."
- "Honestly, I woke up in a really good mood—I don't want to come to work and ruin it."
- "My dog ate my work schedule."[13]

Excuses are often more entertaining than

informative, especially the more "creative" ones. After all, an excuse usually sounds far more believable and reasonable to the person saying it than to the person hearing it. People can usually see right through a flimsy excuse.

One of the funniest verses in the Bible is a flimsy excuse found in Proverbs 22:13 (a similar sentiment is repeated in Proverbs 26:13). It reads, "The lazy person says, 'There's a lion outside! I might get killed out in the street!' " (NCV).

In other words, the person who is trying to avoid work says it is way too risky to go into the big, scary world because he thinks, *What if I go out there and a lion eats me?*

It's such a bad excuse that it's funny.

But King Solomon preserved this proverb for a reason. It represents a universal truth: when we don't want to do something, we come up with excuses. And those excuses sound perfectly reasonable to us, even if they are weak and transparent to everyone else.

The lion-avoiding man gave a reason why he wasn't going out and trying, but it wasn't the *real* reason. Have you checked your own thinking to make sure you aren't making excuses too? There are often real reasons and obstacles that hold us back from pursuing our dreams, but sometimes we use excuses as a way to make ourselves feel better because we didn't do the work.

I've heard it said that you can have excuses or you

can have success—but you can't have both. Excuses and success can't coexist. You can't achieve your goal while simultaneously making an excuse for why you can't achieve your goal.

Excuses may take the pressure off in the short term, but in the long term, they are disempowering. Excuses leave you feeling helpless and incapable, like all the dreams-come-true are for other people, not you. It's time to take a mental inventory. Think about the reasons why you haven't made progress on your dreams and goals. Are you holding on to any flimsy excuses? Pray for insight and courage. As you review your reasons, you might find that some of them are just fears you've imagined, like lions in the road.

Little by little

When the Israelites were slaves in Egypt, God had a plan for them to experience freedom and a fresh start. He knew it would take time. He knew they would be impatient and unable to imagine a life outside of what they had always known. So He gave them promises, provisions, and leaders to help them through the long transition from slavery to freedom.

When God told them which land would eventually become their home, they were confused, because that land was already taken: it was home to some powerful, intimidating people. And those people weren't especially interested in sharing the land. There was no place for the Israelites in their neighborhoods. But God made this promise to them: "I will make all your enemies turn their backs and run. I will send the hornet ahead of you to drive the Hivites, Canaanites and Hittites out of your way" (Exodus 23:27, 28).

That certainly sounded good to the Israelites. They were ready for God to move forward and give them the land immediately. It was an ambitious plan, so they would understand if they had to wait a few weeks or a few months, but they didn't want to drag it out. Surely God understood that they needed a home . . . *now*.

But God knows that sometimes we need time and space between the promise and the fulfillment. Sometimes we need to pause so we'll be ready for bigger things. This was the case with the Israelites. God told them He would move their enemies and obstacles out of the way, but He went on to explain that He wouldn't do it overnight. He said, "But I will not drive them out in a single year, because the land would become desolate and the wild animals too numerous for you. *Little by little* I will drive them out before you, until you have increased enough to take possession of the land" (Exodus 23:29, 30; emphasis added).

Sometimes God takes us to bigger, better places *little by little*. Those are His words: "Little by little." He told the Israelites they couldn't handle a huge dream fulfilled all at once. They wouldn't be able to immediately manage all the territory, and the wild animals would become out of control in the vast land. Their dream life came with some big, new responsibilities, and if they weren't ready to take on those responsibilities, the dream would become a nightmare.

Maybe you, too, will be better off if your dreams come true little by little. Maybe you would be overwhelmed if your life suddenly changed. In your case, it's not literal wild animals and desolate land that stand in your way— but your path will have challenges of its own. Just as God took His time handing over the land to the Israelites, He may be delivering your dreams "little by little" so that you will be strong, ready, and grateful.

Don't give up hope if things aren't happening as quickly as you would like. When the timing is right rather than rushed, you'll be able to fully enjoy the thrill and beauty of a dream come true.

---

1. Emmie Martin, "Nicolas Cage Blew $150 Million on a Dinosaur skull, Pygmy Heads and 2 European Castles," CNBC, updated January 25, 2021, https://www.cnbc.com/2019/08/09/why-nicholas-cage -blew-150-million-dollars-on-a-dinosaur-skull-and-two-castles .html?utm_content=makeit&utm_medium=Social&utm _source=Facebook&fbclid=IwAR3l1bXxDAl94eS39F3q491a Lo8uL3D6P3-Zm8KeCbXyzzmLzE0bpoLTdx4#Echobox =1642538382.

2. Christine Yaged, "How Nicolas Cage Wildly Spent a $150 Million Fortune," FinanceBuzz, updated February 6, 2023, https:// financebuzz.com/finance-nicolas-cage-buying-spree.

3. Yaged.

4. Emmie Martin, "Nicolas Cage Once Blew $150 Million on a Private Island and a Dinosaur Skull—Here's Everything He Bought," CNBC, updated July 5, 2018, https://www.cnbc .com/2018/01/19/how-nicholas-cage-once-blew-his-entire-150 -million-fortune.html.

5. Zoya Gervis, "The Average American Abandons Their New Year's Resolution by This Date," *New York Post*, January 28, 2020, https://nypost.com/2020/01/28/the-average-american-abandons -their-new-years-resolution-by-this-date/.

6. Jon Acuff, "All It Takes Is a Goal," Jon Acuff, accessed June 29, 2023, https://acuff.me/all-it-takes-is-a-goal-book/.

7. Kevin Kruse, "The 80/20 Rule and How It Can Change Your Life," *Forbes*, March 7, 2016, https://www.forbes.com/sites/kevinkruse /2016/03/07/80-20-rule/?sh=364f8f683814.

8. Kruse.

9. Kruse.

10. Kruse.

11. Henry Van Dyke quoted in *Reader's Digest*, December 1960 in *The Reader's Digest Treasury of Modern Quotations* (New York: Thomas Y. Cromwell, 1975), 522.

12. Morten L. Kringelbach, Alan Stein, and Eloise Stark, "How Cute Things Hijack Our Brains and Drive Behaviour," The Conversation, July 4, 2016, https://theconversation.com /how-cute-things-hijack-our-brains-and-drive-behaviour-61942.

13. Adapted from Brandon Specktor, "The 60 Most Ridiculous Excuses People Actually Used to Get Out of Work," *Reader's Digest*, updated February 14, 2023, https://www.rd.com/list/excuses-for -calling-out-of-work/.

CHAPTER 9

Don't Give Up on People

The art of love . . . is largely the art of persistence.
—Albert Ellis

Jim knew he might die, but he got into the small plane anyway.[1]

For months, Jim and four other men had been preparing for this short flight over the thick jungle of Ecuador. Their goal was to visit the Aucas, a dangerous tribe that had killed every outsider who had ever entered their area of the jungle. It seemed reckless to everyone else, but to these men, the mission seemed worth the risk: they wanted to tell the tribe about Jesus. Prior to this, Jim had moved to Ecuador to start a ministry in the jungle.[2] Soon after, Jim married Elisabeth.[3] The newlyweds, along with their mission partners, learned a new language and settled in a small village, immersing themselves in the ways and daily life of the Quechuas, a friendly tribe that welcomed them.[4]

But Jim wasn't content to stop there. He felt a longing to go deeper into the jungle to help the fierce, isolated Auca tribe. So he and four other missionaries came up with a plan to show the Aucas that they had good intentions. While their wives stayed at the mission headquarters near the friendly Quechuas, the men used their small plane to fly over the Auca village and drop gifts and supplies for them.[5]

After several gift-giving expeditions, the missionaries still had not made face-to-face contact with the tribe. But one day the Aucas finally seemed to offer a sign of peace: they left a gift for the missionaries. This gesture convinced the missionaries it was time to meet the tribe.[6]

Finally, after careful planning, they arrived on a beach near the Auca village, where one man and two women from the tribe came out to meet them. They all shared a meal together, and the missionaries even took the man from the tribe for a flight in their plane. After the pleasant interaction, the missionaries asked the Aucas to bring others from their tribe.[7]

The missionaries waited, hoping to meet more Aucas. But before the missionaries knew what was happening, they heard a terrifying cry. Auca warriors with raised spears charged out of the dense trees. Within seconds, the tribesmen threw their spears and killed all five missionaries.[8]

The violent death of the missionaries could have been the end of the dream to build a friendship with the Aucas, but it wasn't. Approximately two years later, Jim's wife, Elisabeth Elliot, along with their young daughter and the sister of one of the other missionaries, returned to that Auca village. Elisabeth didn't do just a quick flyover and drop gifts from a plane. She *moved* to their village.[9] She lived with the very people who had killed her husband. She was determined that God had not given up on the tribe, so she wouldn't either.

Because of her never-give-up love, the tribe is now friendly and many of them are Christians.[10] In addition, they are no longer known by the name Auca, which means "naked savages," a name given to them by their enemies. They now go by the name Waodani, which means "true people."

Holding on to hope instead of a grudge

No one would have blamed Elisabeth if she had packed her bags, taken her young daughter back to the United States, and never returned to the jungles of Ecuador. It would have been perfectly understandable if she had given up on the tribe. But the young widow straightened her back, set her focus, and marched into a scary situation: extending love to people who might not love her back. That's a vulnerable place for anyone to be, but in her case, the stakes were high. If they didn't reciprocate, she wouldn't just end up embarrassed and rejected. She would end up dead.

If anyone had an excuse to give up on someone, it was Elisabeth Elliot. The people had killed her husband. Most people can hold a grudge for far less than that.

- We give up on people when they are rude.
- We give up on people when they keep making the same mistakes.
- We give up on people when they disappoint us.

Don't Give Up on People

- We give up on people when they annoy us.
- We give up on people when they aren't as smart or accomplished as we think they should be.
- We give up on people when they are difficult to love.

If you spend enough time scrolling through social media, you might get the feeling that people are disposable. There will always be a "good vibes only" social media influencer reminding you that if someone annoys you, "You don't need that kind of negativity in your life!" They'll tell you that if someone thinks, votes, or lives differently than you do, you should get rid of that negative energy.

People can be difficult, it's true. But if you discard everyone who is flawed, you'll eventually find yourself alone—because everyone is flawed. Then when you are left alone, finally free of all those flawed people, you'll find that you don't really like yourself that much either—because you, too, are flawed.

While we sometimes give up on people because they aren't enough like us, at other times we give up on them because they are *too much* like us. As I heard an old farmer say one time when describing someone he didn't get along with but who was quite similar to him, "There's something about that boy I don't like about me." Often without realizing it, another person's insecurities, selfishness, or bad habits remind us of negative traits that we have too.

If you're a dog lover, you've likely heard the saying, "The more people I meet, the more I like my dog." After all, it's a lot easier to love an animal than a person, because dogs don't betray, hurt, compete, compare, disappoint, gossip, insult, or say rude things. People, on the other hand, are more complicated. It requires patience and kindness to see the best in them. If you intend not to give up on them, you can't be selfish, proud, or jealous. You can't get upset all the time. You can't keep track of all the times they mess up. You have to keep accepting them the way they are and hoping for even better things for them.

And when you do all of those things, that is the very definition of love, according to the apostle Paul:

> Love is patient and kind. Love is not jealous, it does not brag, and it is not proud. Love is not rude, is not selfish, and does not get upset with others. Love does not count up wrongs that have been done. Love takes no pleasure in evil but rejoices over the truth. Love patiently accepts all things. It always trusts, always hopes, and always endures.
>
> Love never ends (1 Corinthians 13:4–8, NCV).

You'll notice that part of Paul's description of how to love is to always hope. To hold on to hope for someone is a way of loving them. There will be times when they may not have hope for themselves, but you can cling to it for them by praying for them and encouraging them.

Of course, to choose the path of love does not mean you stay in relationships that are abusive or dangerous. The call to love doesn't force you to be tangled up in manipulative, dysfunctional, or abusive relationships. It's possible to hold on to hope while loving someone from a distance.

Ultimately, to hold on to hope for someone is to see them as God sees them: a beloved person with value and worth, potential and possibility. Just like a crushed blade of grass or a dim candle, they might not be at their best, but God sees the best in them.

He sees you that way too: full of value, worth, potential, and possibility, even when you feel crushed and broken.

Jesus, who loves you and all the people you are trying to love, summed it all up this way: "My command is this: Love each other as I have loved you" (John 15:12).

Do you hate people?

I remember seeing an advice column that addressed the increasingly common complaint of "I hate people." The author explained that this trend is more than just feeling annoyed or frustrated with a few people; instead, a growing number of people are making the sweeping declaration that they hate people, all of them. A combination of anger, polarization, depression, past hurts, and social anxiety leads people to believe solitude is better than togetherness.

Choosing to disregard people might seem like a case of "it's their loss, not mine," but it takes a toll on you too, depleting your reserve of emotional energy. Constantly carrying distressing feelings, like disappointment and resentment toward people, often leads to social withdrawal and prompts us to try self-soothing behaviors, such as binging on comfort foods, alcohol, or media. In the long term, this chronic stress and isolation sets off an array of negative consequences for physical, mental, and spiritual health.

In 1938, researchers began what has become the longest-running study on human happiness.[11] The goal of the Harvard Study of Adult Development was to find out the key to a good life. For decades, researchers checked in with participants, investigating all aspects of their lives.[12]

The study found that there was, in fact, one thing in particular that led to increased happiness, greater health, and even a longer life. Despite what you might expect, the key to a happy, healthy life wasn't money, success, exercise, or a healthy diet. The happiest, healthiest participants all had one thing in common: *positive relationships*.[13]

Before you think those participants were lucky and happened to be surrounded by especially wonderful people, remember that they, like you, had ordinary, flawed people in their lives. Here's what sets people with positive relationships apart from those without them: the people with good relationships don't give up on people. They learn how to nurture relationships and live in community even if they get their feelings hurt, experience disappointments, or have misunderstandings. They find people they connect with or have something in common with, and then they stick around long enough to create more positive memories than negative ones.

Looking for the best in people is good for you and for others, because you need them, and they need you. When we hold on to hope, we keep others' best traits in mind and do not focus only on their worst qualities. There's a temptation, especially with people we have known a long time, to assume that "they are who they are," by which we mean they are never going to change. But if you believe in the gospel, you have to believe that people can grow, learn, and change. As Philippians 1:6 reminds us, God is still working on all of us and isn't going to give up: "And I am sure of this, that he who began a good work in you will bring it to completion at the day of Jesus Christ" (ESV).

When it comes to people, don't give up. God is still working. He is right in the middle of doing a good work in all of us, including in you and the people around you. If God can see beauty and possibility in trampled grass, dim candles, and broken people, surely, if we try, we can catch a glimpse of hope too.

1. Tim Chester, "Jim Elliot Was No Fool," Crossway, January 28, 2018, https://www.crossway.org/articles/jim-elliot-was-no-fool/.

2. "Jim Elliot: Story and Legacy," Christianity.com, June 5, 2020, https://www.christianity.com/church/church-history/timeline/1901-2000/jim-elliot-no-fool-11634862.html.

3. "Elisabeth Elliot: The Missionary Who Lived With the Tribe That Killed Her Husband," New Life Publishing, accessed August 9, 2023, https://www.newlifepublishing.co.uk/articles/faith/elisabeth-elliot-the-missionary-who-lived-with-the-tribe-that-killed-her-husband/.

4. "Jim Elliot."

5. "Jim Elliot."

6. "Jim Elliot."

7. "Jim Elliot."

8. "Jim Elliot."

9. "Elisabeth Elliot."

10. "Elisabeth Elliot."

11. Robert Waldinger and Marc Schulz, "What the Longest Study on Human Happiness Found Is the Key to a Good Life," *The Atlantic*, January 19, 2023, https://www.theatlantic.com/ideas/archive/2023/01/harvard-happiness-study-relationships/672753/.

12. Marc Schulz and Robert Waldinger, "An 85-Year Harvard Study Found the No. 1 Thing That Makes Us Happy in Life: It Helps Us 'Live Longer,' " CNBC, February 10, 2023, https://www.cnbc.com/2023/02/10/85-year-harvard-study-found-the-secret-to-a-long-happy-and-successful-life.html#:~:text=The%20most%20consistent%20finding%20we,and%20help%20us%20live%20longer.

13. Schulz and Waldinger.

CHAPTER 10

Don't Give Up on Your Health and Well-Being

Dear friend, I pray that you may enjoy good health and that all may go well with you, even as your soul is getting along well.
—3 John 1:2

If you drive on the dirt road just outside of Crested Butte, Colorado, you'll find yourself on Kebler Pass. And if you drive that dirt road during autumn, you'll find yourself in awe. For miles and miles, you'll be surrounded by a massive aspen grove bursting with bright yellow leaves.

The trees are all perfectly synchronized: the leaves on every tree appear at the same time in spring, and the trees change colors simultaneously each fall. That's because the aspen trees on Kebler Pass are all connected by a single root system, making the grove one of the largest living organisms in the nation.[1]

Alone, each tree is beautiful. Together they are magnificent. And it all starts with an interconnectedness that is underground, out of sight.

Like the trees in an aspen grove, your mind, body, and spirit are woven together in ways you cannot see. That's why a change—for good or bad—in your mental, physical, or spiritual health will influence all the other areas of your health. For example, receiving a hug may reduce pain, lower your stress level, and decrease your chances of getting sick.[2] That's just one of many ways that our interconnectedness is positive. But the connection of your mind and body can also have a negative impact. For example, when you are worried and stressed about a work deadline, your blood pressure can spike. Or if you're feeling nervous, you might get shortness of breath or an upset stomach.

Everything within you is connected. Your activity level, your emotions, your food choices, your thoughts all affect you in ways you may not be able to see or even imagine. When this interconnection creates positive results, it is one of the things that makes you magnificent, even more magnificent than an interconnected aspen grove.

The mind is a powerful thing

Diet and exercise. For many people, this phrase immediately comes to mind when they think about health. They imagine endless, joyless days of salads and gym classes. But health, of course, isn't just what you eat or how far you can run. In fact, focusing *only* on the body can leave you constantly chasing after gimmicks and empty promises like "Get a beach body in thirty days" or "Lose twenty pounds in two weeks."

Pursuing health is different than pursuing the *appearance* of health. For example, a person might be thin or physically strong, but if they are lonely and feel like life is meaningless, then they aren't entirely healthy. If you focus on only one part of the mind-body-spirit trio, you can end up neglecting other major aspects of your health.

So as we explore the topic of health, let's not focus only on the body. In fact, let's start by talking about the mind.

One of the great mysteries related to the mind-body connection is the placebo effect.

A placebo is an inactive drug or treatment that has no properties that would cause physical changes, yet placebos have been shown to bring about a variety of positive physical results. For example, in studies where participants receive a placebo pill, thinking they are getting treatment for a health problem, some people actually experience improvements like reduced pain, improved blood pressure, lowered heart rate,[3] and increased relaxation.[4] The improvements aren't brought about by the fake treatment, so the only explanation is that the improvement come from the patients' *belief* in the treatment.[5]

The opposite of the placebo effect is true too. The "nocebo effect" leads people to experience negative symptoms due to the expectation of negative outcomes. For example, when participants in studies are given placebo pills and told that a headache is a common side effect of that medicine, they are more likely to report headaches after taking the pill. The word *placebo* comes from the Latin "I shall please," while *nocebo* comes from the Latin "I shall harm." Both experiences prove the same thing: the power of our expectations. If you have decided in your mind that something is going to help, you're probably going to notice improvement. And if you expect that something is going to harm you, you're more likely to experience it that way.[6]

Your expectations influence your results.

When it comes to your health, your expectations matter far more than you realize. If you think you'll never be able to get active, lose weight, or feel joyful again, then you're setting yourself up for the very outcome you fear. But when you *expect* a good outcome, your body releases feel-good neurotransmitters, like endorphins and dopamine, and your brain lights up in the areas that improve your mood and raise your self-awareness.

Simply put, *believing* you can be healthier makes it more likely that you will be.

Give yourself a placebo

Of course, we know a placebo can work when someone doesn't know it's a placebo. But interestingly, according to a study, a placebo can also be helpful even when people *know* they're getting one. In a study of people who suffered from migraines, one group of participants was given a migraine drug, another group took a pill labeled "placebo," and the third group took no medication. It turns out that the placebo was fifty percent as effective at reducing migraine pain as the actual drug.[7] That's incredible results for a pill that had no medicinal power.

That migraine study proves that you don't have to be tricked into experiencing the placebo effect. You can give yourself a placebo. For example, you probably already know that taking regular walks is good for you. (It aids in weight loss and helps prevent heart disease, diabetes, cancer, stroke, and high blood pressure. Walking also improves your mood, memory, sleep, energy levels, balance, and coordination.[8]) Now, add the placebo effect and *expect* the walks to have good results, and you multiply the positive impact. By telling yourself that the walk will make you feel better and will be good for you, your mind convinces your body that this is, in fact, going to be good—very good.

Healing your spirit

Your mind isn't the only thing that influences your overall health. Your spirit does too.

Throughout history, religion and medicine have been closely intertwined. In fact, during the Middle Ages and up through the French Revolution, if you called for a doctor, the person who arrived at your door would likely be the same person who would have shown up if you had called for a clergyman.[9] Even in the American colonies, many of the physicians were also clergy.[10]

It is only in recent times that religion and medicine have been considered separate systems of healing rather than one unified system. Especially in modern, developed countries in the West, spirituality and health care are now treated separately, even though historically they have been connected. In fact, the first hospitals in the West were built by religious organizations and staffed by religious orders.[11]

Interestingly, health care is increasingly returning to its

roots: reuniting a person's health and spirituality. Dr. Tracy Balboni, the lead author of what is considered one of the most comprehensive studies of modern literature on health and spirituality, says, "Our findings indicate that attention to spirituality in serious illness and in health should be a vital part of future whole person–centered care."[12]

Healthy spirit, healthy body

Think back to a time in your life when your spirit felt crushed. A time where you were experiencing overwhelming grief, rejection, disappointment, or fear. Maybe you experienced the death of a loved one, went through a heartbreaking divorce, or lost your job. Whatever happened, it left you feeling like a part of your spirit was wounded. During that time, you likely felt physically drained. You probably wanted to crawl back into bed, and, if I had to guess, your food cravings leaned more toward mac and cheese and ice cream than brussels sprouts and beets. Because your spirit was drained, your body felt weak and worn down.

Thousands of years ago, King Solomon wrote, "A cheerful heart is good medicine, but a broken spirit saps a person's strength" (Proverbs 17:22, NLT). No surprise that modern research supports this ancient wisdom. There's an undeniable connection between your spiritual health and your overall health. Consider just some of the findings about how the state of your spirit affects your body:

- People who frequently attend religious services live

37 percent longer than those who don't attend. In fact, going to church prolongs a person's life span as much as cholesterol-reducing drugs.[13]

- Having an active spiritual life boosts your immune system, increasing the body's levels of infection-fighting white blood cells and T cells.[14]
- Patients with Alzheimer's disease keep their cognitive and behavioral function longer if they are highly spiritual. The less religious they are, the quicker they experience decline.[15]
- Religious people have a 75 percent lower risk of suffering from major depression than nonreligious people.[16]
- Spiritual people tend to have healthier habits: they are more likely to exercise, eat healthfully, have social support, and they are less likely to smoke and drink alcohol.[17]

All of these facts about the interconnectedness of our mind, body, and spirit remind us that whenever we are pursuing better health, it's not just about physical changes. We have to get our head and heart involved too.

Start now; it's not too late

If you've ever promised yourself that you would start a diet on Monday or make a healthy change tomorrow but didn't follow through, you are not alone. As I heard one discouraged person say, "It feels like adulthood is just years of breaking promises to myself."

95

We break our promises to ourselves so often that we don't even believe ourselves anymore when we say we're going to do something. But here is the good news: God doesn't break His promises. And He promised that He would complete the good work He began in you (Philippians 1:6).

When we don't follow through on what we planned, we might assume God isn't going to keep His word either. But in Psalm 50:21, God speaks up, explaining that we are mistaken about Him. "You thought I was exactly like you," He says. In other words, God is saying that just because we break our promises, that doesn't mean He does too.

Just like a crushed blade of grass or a dim candle, your half-finished, half-hearted attempts won't make Him give up. He will keep His promise to see you through.

If you need an inspiring reason to pick up any abandoned dreams for a healthier, happier life, this is it: the never-give-up God is cheering for you and is still fully committed to helping you. Whether you want to lose weight, eat healthier, stop smoking, increase your joy, or strengthen your body, it's not too late to move forward with your goal. He won't get you halfway there and then abandon you.

Even if you didn't make healthy choices in the past, that doesn't mean you can't make them now. As the old saying goes, "The best time to plant a tree was twenty years ago. The second best time is now." Right now is a perfectly good time to begin. Don't let past regrets or defeats hold you back.

In fact, research supports the fact that it's not too late. For example, a study found that people who start exercising in their forties or fifties "reduce their mortality risk just as much as people who've been exercising their whole lives as compared to folks who are completely sedentary."[18] In other words, the best time was twenty years ago. The second-best time is now.

How to be healthier and happier

As the senior editor of the health magazine *Vibrant Life*, I've seen a lot of expert health advice cross my desk. There are countless suggestions and opinions, and while one expert promotes one thing, another will insist on the opposite.

Instead of getting caught up in fads or unproven claims, let's stick to the simple, timeless truths. Whether you are experiencing peak health or struggling to just get by, there are health principles that will help you take steps toward better health.

Whatever your starting point or end goal may be, here are some things you can begin doing today to improve your health and well-being:

- *Go easy on yourself.*

  Self-criticism is not self-motivation. In fact, it is the opposite. Beating yourself up when you have a setback will actually leave you feeling *less* motivated and hopeful. It is far more effective to show yourself compassion than to be hard on yourself.

Self-compassion doesn't mean you are a quitter or that you are self-indulgent and lazy. It means you will be kind to yourself when you face your shortcomings. Studies have found that when you show self-directed compassion, you'll experience a wave of improvements, including increased optimism,[19] better physical and mental health,[20] reduced fear of failure, heightened connectedness and curiosity, and less depression and anxiety.[21]

Go easy on yourself as you form new habits. Self-criticism causes you to lose hope and give up, but self-compassion makes it easier to try again tomorrow.

- *Make a plan, not a wish.*

  There's a childlike sweetness to making a wish when you see a shooting star or when you blow out a birthday candle, but there's a deep, life-changing satisfaction to making a *plan*. I've never met a person who achieved their goals merely by wishing for them. But a plan? A plan can turn a wish into a reality.

  When you want to improve your health, you need a plan, and a plan starts with goals. To ensure success, choose goals that are specific and realistic:

  Specific—Instead of setting the vague intention to "eat healthier," set a specific goal, such as "fill two-thirds of my plate with vegetables and fruit." Instead of "exercise more," get detailed and aim for something like "walk thirty minutes a day, five days a week." When you have a specific goal, it becomes measurable and manageable. You become clear on the goal and can keep track of your progress on your phone or in a journal. You can see day by day how you're doing.

Realistic—Let's say it's June 1, and you're looking forward to a beach vacation at the end of July. You want to lose fifty pounds, and you want it to happen quickly, before your sunshiny getaway. But that goal isn't realistic, so you're setting yourself up for disappointment and failure. Stick with healthy, reasonable goals instead, and tackle them with slow and steady progress.

Make sure your goal fits the resources, schedule, and information you have. If you make it a goal to go to the gym for one hour every day after work, but the scheduling often conflicts with taking your children to their extracurricular activities, the goal isn't going to work, which will cause you to give up.

To make sure your goal is the right fit, do research, join an online group, or ask for advice from someone you trust and respect. Sometimes the people closest to you can give invaluable insight, suggestions, and support.

- *Take a walk.*
  Wouldn't it be nice if there were a magic pill

that would help you lose weight, have more energy, live longer, get stronger, unlock creativity, combat depression, lower your cholesterol, improve your blood pressure, and lower your risk of heart disease, diabetes, and cancer? And since this pill is magic, it would, of course, be totally free and have no side effects. It sounds too good to be true, but these are exactly the benefits of walking. That's why some doctors, in fact, call walking "the magic pill."[22]

Whatever your health goal is, walking will help. If you want to strengthen your body, clear your mind, or calm your spirit, it helps in all those ways and more. It doesn't have the adventurous reputation of other physical activities, like running, cycling, or rock climbing, but don't let that fool you. Walking has first-rate results.

Honestly, some of us owe walking an apology. We've underestimated it and overlooked it, dismissing it as a boring, insignificant activity. But walking becomes hiking if you do it on a trail in nature. (See, it already sounds more interesting, doesn't it?) Walking also becomes a social activity if you invite a friend. And when you do it regularly, walking becomes medicine.

• *Focus on adding, not subtracting.*
Sometimes the motivation to make a healthy change is that you're totally, finally fed up with

the way things are. You're tired of carrying extra weight, or not having enough energy, or getting bad news from your doctor. So your mind goes to the things you need to change, including all the things you want to stop doing, such as smoking, overeating, or drinking alcohol. In a burst of frustration and fresh starts, you decide to stop. And maybe you do for a while, but then you pick it back up because giving it up created a void that you didn't fill with something else.

Instead of focusing on *subtracting* things, focus on *adding* things. In other words, create good habits that crowd out the old habits. For example, let's say you drink six sodas a day, and you want to quit. Rather than setting a goal to eliminate soda, start with a goal of drinking eight glasses of water every day. Once you're doing that, you'll be so full of water that you probably won't want your usual six sodas. You're crowding out the soda. If those sodas were also a midmorning or midafternoon pick-me-up, take a brisk walk instead of reaching for a soda. As you add new routines, you'll crowd out bad habits with better habits.

- *Let nature nurture you.*
  There's a reason why strolling on the beach is more calming than being stuck in traffic, or why walking through a meadow is more relaxing than sitting in a windowless office. Nature has a way of

soothing our spirits and calming our nerves, and when we're immersed in nature, it helps us heal.

The great outdoors offers a number of health benefits, including better immune system function, lower blood pressure, healthier self-esteem, reduced aggression,[23] improved mood, lower stress levels, an increased sense of empathy and cooperation, reduced anxiety, and decreased feelings of isolation.[24] In addition, there is a theory that "nature replenishes one's cognitive resources, restoring the ability to concentrate and pay attention."[25] The health benefits are so undeniable that an increasing number of physicians are even "prescribing" nature to their patients, encouraging time outdoors as part of their approach to health and wellness.[26]

Research has discovered that "green spaces" (areas filled with grass and trees) and "blue spaces" (areas with features such as rivers, oceans, and lakes) are especially good for our mental health.[27] And exposure to these natural settings early in life brings a lifetime of benefits. People who grow up with very little or no green space nearby have as much as a 55 percent greater risk of developing problems like depression, anxiety, and substance abuse later in life.[28]

Fortunately, you don't have to pack a bag and go to the ocean or the mountains to enjoy the power of green spaces and blue spaces. You can get the same health boost close to home: in a city park, near a pond, or in a patch of trees. Studies suggest that spending at least two hours each week outside will help you achieve significant benefits to your health and well-being.[29] That adds up to just a little more than seventeen minutes a day. And if you take a walk during those seventeen minutes, you'll accomplish two health goals at once.

- *Don't make your first thought your worst thought.*
  On average, a person has more than six thousand thoughts per day. That means every nine seconds you transition to a new thought.[30] Each idea might last only a short time, but all of them together influence every aspect of your life, including your emotions, mood, behavior, and relationships.

  Nine seconds at a time, your thoughts are making you who you are. While some of those thoughts are everyday musings (like deciding what to wear or which cereal to eat), other thoughts play a more significant role. In particular, your first thoughts in the morning help determine the tone of your day.

  If you awaken to thoughts of dread or defeat, then other thoughts will follow in that direction. And as those thoughts convince you that today is going to be a bad day, you may get a sinking feeling, leaving you with the overwhelming desire to roll over and stay in bed.

Fortunately, you can choose your thoughts instead of letting them choose you. The Bible repeatedly encourages us to make sure our first thoughts of the day are positive ones:

o "In the morning I will sing of your love" (Psalm 59:16).
o "In the morning my prayer comes before you" (Psalm 88:13).
o "In the morning my spirit longs for you" (Isaiah 26:9).
o "Satisfy us in the morning with your unfailing love" (Psalm 90:14).
o "Let me hear Your loving-kindness in the morning" (Psalm 143:8, NLV).

When you wake up and immediately pick up your phone to scroll through news that makes you feel unsettled or social media posts that leave you feeling inadequate and jealous, you've allowed your first thoughts to be your worst thoughts. Instead, when you wake up—before you even open your eyes—bring your mind to a hopeful place. Create a first-thought habit, such as reciting a Bible verse, saying a prayer over your day, or listing three things you're thankful for.

Healthy hopes

Over the years, I've heard a lot of stories of people who have made major improvements to their health. Whether they stopped smoking, lost weight, changed their diet, or transformed from a couch potato to a marathon runner, they all experienced results that they once thought impossible. Everyone's path to better health is different, but there's one thing people often say helped them get healthier: faith in God. They've found that praying and turning to God as a source of strength gives them the determination and courage to keep trying.

The prophecy of the never-give-up God helps put things in perspective. If God can see potential in crushed grass and dim candles, He definitely sees potential in you. He wants you to experience a healthy, abundant life. He hasn't given up on that goal, so you shouldn't either.

1. Jessica Hughes, "Experience the Fall Colors of Kebler Pass," *Uncover Colorado* (blog), Uncover Colorado, September 6, 2021, https://www.uncovercolorado.com/kebler-pass-aspen-grove/.

2. "Can You Kiss and Hug Your Way to Better Health? Research Says Yes," *Health and Wellness* (blog), Penn Medicine, January 8, 2018, https://www.pennmedicine.org/updates/blogs/health-and-wellness/2018/february/affection.

3. Robert H. Shmerling, "The Placebo Effect: Amazing and Real," *Harvard Health Blog*, Harvard Health Publishing, June 22, 2020, https://www.health.harvard.edu/blog/the-placebo-effect-amazing-and-real-201511028544.

4. "The Power of the Placebo Effect," Mental Health, Harvard Health Publishing, December 13, 2021, https://www.health.harvard.edu/mental-health/the-power-of-the-placebo-effect#:~:text=%22Placebos%20may%20make%20you%20feel,effects%20like%20fatigue%20and%20nausea.%22.

5. Shmerling, "Placebo Effect."

6. Shmerling.

7. "Power of the Placebo Effect."

8. Mayo Clinic Staff, "Walking: Trim Your Waistline, Improve Your Health," Healthy Lifestyle, Mayo Clinic, May 19, 2021, https://www.mayoclinic.org/healthy-lifestyle/fitness/in-depth/walking/art-20046261.

9. Daniel E. Hall, "Altar and Table: A Phenomenology of the Surgeon-Priest," *Yale Journal of Biology and Medicine* 81, no. 4 (December 2008): 193–198, https://www.ncbi.nlm.nih.gov/pmc/articles/PMC2605310/.

10. Patricia A. Watson, *The Angelical Conjunction: The Preacher-Physicians of Colonial New England* (Knoxville, TN: University of Tennessee Press, 1991), 3.

11. Johan Tangelder, "A History of Healthcare . . . and Why Christians Have Done It Different," *Reformed Perspective*, September 21, 2018, https://reformedperspective.ca/a-history-of-healthcare-and-why-christians-have-done-it-different/.

12. "Spirituality Linked With Better Health Outcomes, Patient Care," Harvard T.H. Chan School of Public Health, July 12, 2022, https://www.hsph.harvard.edu/news/press-releases/spirituality-better-health-outcomes-patient-care/.

13. Harold G. Koenig, "Religion, Spirituality, and Health: The Research and Clinical Implications," *International Scholarly Research Notices*, (2012), https://doi.org/10.5402/2012/278730.

14. Koenig.

15. A. Coin et al., "Does Religiosity Protect Against Cognitive and Behavioral Decline in Alzheimers Dementia?," *Current Alzheimer Research* 7, no. 5 (2010): 445–452, https://doi.org/10.2174/156720510791383886.

16. Lisa Miller et al., "Religiosity and Major Depression in Adults at High Risk: A Ten-Year Prospective Study," *American Journal of Psychiatry* 169, no. 1 (January 2012): 89–94, https://doi.org/10.1176/appi.ajp.2011.10121823.

17. Koenig, "Religion."

18. Sara Chodosh, "Late-Blooming Exercisers May Get the Same Benefits as Lifelong Gym Rats," *Popular Science*, March 9, 2019, https://www.popsci.com/older-adults-start-exercising/.

19. Kristin D. Neff, "The Role of Self-Compassion in Development:

A Healthier Way to Relate to Oneself," *Human Development* 52, no. 4 (2009): 211–214, https://doi.org/10.1159/000215071.

20. Kristin J. Homan and Fuschia M. Sirois, "Self-Compassion and Physical Health: Exploring the Roles of Perceived Stress and Health-Promoting Behaviors," *Health Psychology Open* 4, no. 2 (July–December 2017): 1–9, https://doi.org/10.1177/2055102917729542.

21. Kristin D. Neff, "Self-Compassion," in *Handbook of Individual Differences in Social Behavior*, ed. Mark R. Leary and Rick H. Hoyle (New York: Guilford Press: 2009), 570, 571.

22. Kay Hawes, "The Magic Pill," *Kansas Medicine + Science*, Spring–Summer 2023, https://www.kumc.edu/communications/about/publications/kansas-medicine-and-science/spring-summer-2023/the-magic-pill.html.

23. Jim Robbins, "Ecopsychology: How Immersion in Nature Benefits Your Health," *Yale Environment 360*, January 9, 2020, https://e360.yale.edu/features/ecopsychology-how-immersion-in-nature-benefits-your-health.

24. Kirsten Weir, "Nurtured by Nature," *Monitor on Psychology*, April/May 2020, 52, 55, https://www.apa.org/monitor/2020/2020-04-monitor.pdf.

25. Weir, 52.

26. Jillian Mock, "Why Doctors Are Prescribing Nature Walks," *Time*, April 27, 2022, https://time.com/6171174/nature-stress-benefits-doctors/.

27. Carolyn Crist, "Exposure to 'Blue Spaces' Linked to Better Mental Health," WebMD, October 14, 2022, https://www.webmd.com/a-to-z-guides/news/20221014/exposure-blue-spaces-linked-better-mental-health.

28. "Green Space Is Good for Mental Health," NASA Earth Observatory, accessed June 28, 2023, https://earthobservatory.nasa.gov/images/145305/green-space-is-good-for-mental-health.

29. Mathew P. White et al., "Spending at Least 120 Minutes a Week in Nature Is Associated With Good Health and Wellbeing," *Scientific Reports* 9, 7730 (2019): 1–11, https://doi.org/10.1038/s41598-019-44097-3.

30. Crystal Raypole, "How Many Thoughts Do You Have Each Day? And Other Things to Think About," Healthline, February 28, 2022, https://www.healthline.com/health/how-many-thoughts-per-day.

CHAPTER 11

Don't Give Up on Church

We are biologically, cognitively, physically, and spiritually wired to love, to be loved, and to belong. When those needs are not met, we don't function as we were meant to. We break. We fall apart. We numb. We ache. We hurt others. We get sick.
—Brené Brown

It was pitch-black, the middle of the night. Jesus had been under such intense emotional and spiritual demands that He sweat blood. A plan had been set in motion, and He knew it was now hitting a tipping point—there was no turning back. Everything sped toward a dreadful outcome: Jesus would be executed in the cruelest, most brutal way His enemies could devise.

Jesus took His closest friends to their usual spot, a secluded olive grove. And He asked only one thing of them: "Please pray." He went to pray by Himself, just a stone's throw away, but His friends soon fell asleep. Perhaps they started in prayer, but that didn't last long.

When Jesus returned and found them sleeping, He was saddened and disappointed. But this was only the first in a sequence of terrible disappointments that would happen that night.

While Jesus asked His disciples why they rested instead of praying, a crowd approached, led by one of His disciples—Judas. This was a betrayal made even crueler by the familiarity and intimacy of it: Judas approached Jesus and kissed Him on the cheek. What should have been an act of loyalty was used as an act of treachery, a signal to Jesus' enemies. The One who is kissed is the One who will be arrested.

Betrayal, of course, is especially shattering when it comes from the people closest to you, those who have kissed you on the cheek.

With just one question, Jesus pointed out the soullessness of the act, that an action meant to appear loving was used for cruelty: "Judas, are you betraying the Son of Man with a kiss?" (Luke 22:48). Maybe His voice wavered when He asked, or maybe His voice was strong and steady. Either way, no answer was necessary. The question was answered by the fact that there was a crowd of bloodthirsty soldiers, priests, officers, and elders surrounding Jesus with hatred in their eyes.

Yet the disloyalty had only begun. The mob seized Jesus and dragged Him to the house of the high priest. Peter, who normally stayed close to Jesus, intentionally kept his distance, following from afar. Things weren't looking good for Jesus, and Peter didn't want to be too closely associated with Him. Only when someone kindled a fire in the middle of the courtyard did Peter finally slink up and stand near the others.

First a servant girl, then another bystander, and finally a

third person all recognized Peter. "We know you are with this Man!" they each said. And all three times Peter denied knowing Jesus, just as Jesus had predicted he would. Until that night, Peter had been following Jesus like a shadow, but now Peter pretended they'd never even met.

Nearby, Jesus was being guarded like a criminal. He couldn't walk over and address Peter's denials. But after Peter denied Jesus a third time, Jesus did what He could. He made a small gesture, an expression of hurt and love: "The Lord turned and looked straight at Peter" (Luke 22:61). Jesus didn't say a word; He just looked Peter straight in the eye and pierced him with a knowing glance.

It was enough to make Peter fall apart. He rushed away, weeping bitterly.

Jesus heals those hurt by His followers

To summarize Jesus' dreadful evening thus far: His friends didn't do the one simple thing He asked them to do during His deepest time of need. One of His friends placed Him in a deadly situation in exchange for money. And three times another friend publicly pretended not to know Him.

Even so, through all of those disappointing experiences, Jesus stayed calm. He stayed focused. He said very little. But there was one more thing that happened that night, right after Judas's betrayal and before Peter's betrayal. And *that* was the thing that showed where Jesus drew a line.

Think back to the olive grove where Jesus had been

praying while His friends slept. As they rubbed the sleep from their eyes, the disciples saw a murderous mob approaching with torches in their hands and scowls on their faces. These people were not coming to debate the law or ask for a miracle. They were coming for blood.

In an attempt to defend Jesus from these circling enemies, Peter pulled a sword and cut off the ear of Malchus, a servant of the high priest. This mob may have come for a fight, but it was Jesus' follower who threw the first punch.

The bad situation quickly got worse. With chaos and revenge already in the air, now there was also a bleeding man, and his screams of pain stoked the fire of rage.

That night Jesus let things play out naturally without much intervention. But in this case, His friends had crossed the line. Enough was enough. Jesus roared over the madness, "No more of this!" (Luke 22:51).

Jesus hadn't stopped people from hurting Him, but when His followers hurt others in His name, He wouldn't stand for it.

That's the limit for Jesus: when His followers hurt someone in an attempt to defend Him, He stepped in. Not only did He stop it, but He healed the wound.

Luke describes the moment: "But Jesus answered, 'No more of this!' And he touched the man's ear and healed him" (Luke 22:51). This was the final miracle Jesus performed before His death. He could have used the final miracle before His death to *prevent* His death. He could have called down angels, struck His enemies with lightning, vanished into thin air to avoid being arrested. Instead, He chose for His last miracle to be the healing of someone who had been hurt by His followers.

When church hurts instead of heals

In the sword-wielding encounter between Malchus (a man on the side of Jesus' enemies) and Peter (one of Jesus' closest companions on Earth), you might expect Jesus to take His friend's side. But He intervened to help the man who had received the blow from Peter's sword.

Jesus knew, and He knows still, that even His well-meaning followers hurt others. Sometimes it's on purpose, sometimes it's an accident, and sometimes it's in His defense. That is why in that moment, on that dark night, instead of focusing on His own impending death or His followers' fears, He chose to heal a man bleeding and crying out because of a painful strike from a Jesus follower.

There's no way to know how many countless individuals through the years have been hurt by people who claim to be Jesus' followers. In recent times, surveys indicate that millions upon millions of "unchurched" people are actually people who once attended church but gave it up because of pain or hurt they experienced at church.[1] One researcher says that almost everyone who has been part of a church has experienced some kind of "church hurt" at some point, including those who stay connected to a church.[2]

For some people, their church hurt comes from rude

comments, the self-righteous judgments of others, or gossipy hit jobs. For others, the hurt results from feeling left out, overlooked, or unappreciated. In some cases, the church isn't there for someone during a difficult time. For others, the pain is far greater—abusive and reprehensible—and the devastating emotional scars remain.

If you are a person who has been hurt by a follower of Jesus, let the story of Peter and Malchus bring you comfort. Jesus is on your side. He didn't want you to be hurt. He wants you to be healed, and He will be the one to do it.

One big, happy (imperfect) family

While many people give up on organized religion because of emotional pain they experienced within a church, that's not the only reason people leave. Some are skeptical of the beliefs, find the people hypocritical or judgmental, or think church is boring and irrelevant.

Yet, Jesus Himself modeled that a life of faith is a life of community. To follow Jesus means we live in partnership with fellow believers, even though we are all imperfect. Jesus could have accomplished His mission on Earth without the help of coarse fishermen and tradesmen, but He let a bunch of mistake-makers come along for the ride.

I imagine life with Jesus' disciples was a little like baking cookies with a toddler—it's a lot easier to do it without them, but part of the joy comes from teaching them, seeing them delight in the experience, and forming a bond with them. Jesus could have built His ministry on His own. It would have gone a lot smoother without inexperienced people making a mess of things, but He invited them to join Him so they could learn, connect with one another, and feel the wonder of being a part of something special.

Of course, the small community that Jesus built eventually grew, creating an even larger community, ever increasing—even now—to include more and more people throughout the world. When He started the movement, the idea of living in relationship with other God followers didn't seem especially optional—it seemed central.

You may get a sense of belonging and identity from a friend group, a mom group, a club or sport, or your workplace. But there is something distinctly significant about belonging to a spiritual group of people who share your highest hopes and your deepest beliefs. It allows you to transcend other divisions and differences. It teaches you to be in a relationship with people of various backgrounds, ages, races, incomes, and education levels. You no longer are just friends or acquaintances. You become *family*.

It sounds almost like a riddle, but the apostle John describes how we all transition into one family:

> But to all who did receive him, who believed in his name, he gave the right to become children of God, who were born, not of blood nor of the will of the flesh nor of the will of man, but of God.

And the Word became flesh and dwelt among us, and we have seen his glory, glory as of the only Son from the Father, full of grace and truth (John 1:12–14, ESV).

John is reminding us that as babies, we didn't get to choose the family we would be born into. We didn't even choose to be born. But Jesus did choose. And, of all things, he chose to be born into humanity—one big, broken, dysfunctional family. And because He did that, we can choose to be a part of the new family He created. Because He chose to be a child of man, each of us gets to be a child of God.

We need to be totally honest about this idea of becoming family, though. It sounds so sweet and simple to say, "We are the family of God!" But sometimes family members are the most difficult people to get along with. Family relationships can be complicated because of shared history, expectations, resentments, and insecurities. You know one another's weaknesses, vulnerabilities, and mistakes.

As my mom once said when one of our family members was being difficult, "They are challenging, but they are ours." This is family, when we can fill in that sentence with any annoying or negative trait and still end claiming the other person as ours: "They are impatient, but they are ours. They are rude sometimes, but they are ours. They are uninformed on that topic, but they are ours. They make mistakes, but they are ours."

Paul describes the church family in a similar way: "We are many parts of one body, and we all belong to each other" (Romans 12:5, NLT). We all belong to one another. They are ours. And we are theirs.

The church habit

As an increasing number of people give up on church attendance, some have turned to online church services as an alternative. Others forgo church services altogether because they consider themselves "spiritual but not religious." While it's possible to still experience personal spiritual growth with these approaches, you miss out on something irreplaceable that happens when you regularly meet with others of shared faith.

The Bible says Jesus went to the synagogue every Sabbath "*as was his custom*" (Luke 4:16; emphasis added). The same phrase is used to describe Paul's religious habits: "*As was his custom*, Paul went into the synagogue" (Acts 17:2; emphasis added). Certainly, Jesus and Paul could have skipped religious services and used the excuse that they had better things to do or didn't get anything out of it. But they valued the tradition of meeting with and contributing to a community of believers.

Even in the early church, there was the temptation to try to go it alone on the spiritual journey. It was a big enough problem that the letter to the Hebrews reminded the believers to keep getting together, even though some people were giving up: "Let us not give up the habit of meeting together, as some are doing" (Hebrews 10:25, GNT).

I am a pastor's wife, so you might think I wouldn't understand all the reasons people give up on church. Actually, it's quite the opposite. I have seen up close the flaws and mistakes made by churches. I know how church has let people down and failed them in significant ways. I have personally felt hurt and disappointed at times. But I don't give up on church because I also have seen when the church gets it right: when they lavish people with love and when they build one another up, providing a safe place to grow, struggle, serve, and learn.

In a way, a church is like a gym. Both are places filled with people who believe in the importance of something and are in the process of working on it. If I walk into a gym and notice some people exercising who are out of shape, I don't march out of the building and say, "Those people are such hypocrites. They say they believe in health, but they aren't even healthy!" Likewise, we can't walk into a church, notice someone who isn't especially loving or Christlike, and stomp out, shouting, "Those people are such hypocrites! They say they believe in Jesus, but they aren't perfect like Jesus!" Christians are simply people who are in the process, struggling and starting over like people trying to get fit in the gym.

There are times when attending church services is an absolute blessing. You leave feeling spiritually fortified, inspired, and connected to God and others. Other times, church attendance can feel more like a spiritual discipline.

Placing your overstimulated mind and restless spirit in a quiet setting can sometimes seem boring or stifling. Instead of scrolling fast-paced newsfeeds or switching to more stimulating activities, you remain still and you rest from other pursuits. You accept God's invitation: "Be still, and know that I am God" (Psalm 46:10).

Rather than thinking of regular church attendance as a chore, think of it as a vow renewal. It is going to the house of the Lord and recommitting to the teachings of Jesus. It's a weekly declaration that you still intend to follow in the path of Jesus. You renew your commitment to His principles of faith, hope, and love. And through this ritual, you add meaning to your daily life.

Remember, too, that if church lacks something important to you, that might not be a deal-breaker: rather, it might be a call to action. For example, let's say you have a passion for helping teenagers or meeting needs within your city, but you don't see the church doing enough in those areas. If you notice a need and think, *Someone should do something about that*, then that "someone" might just be *you*. You detected the need and have a passion for it, while others walked right past it without a thought. Consider the things you think "someone" should do, and ask yourself if you are that someone.

The blessing of belonging

Not all churches are the same. Each has their own culture, personality, and priorities. Some are unhealthy and dysfunctional and should be avoided, but plenty of them are safe and welcoming.

Don't let past hurts or disappointments keep you from experiencing the benefits of a faith community. If you've been hurt at church, set your eyes on Jesus, who heals those who have been hurt by His followers. If you're frustrated that church sometimes feels more like a business organization or social club than a spiritual movement, let the Lord settle up all the agenda items, membership lists, and financial reports. If you meet people at church who struggle with rudeness or selfishness, don't let them steal your joy. As Jesus told Peter when he was worried about other followers, "What concern is it of yours? You follow me" (John 21:22, NABRE). Don't be so concerned about other followers that you lose sight of following Jesus.

When Christ built up a community here on Earth, His message to everyone who joined Him was, "You are known. You are loved. You belong." None of that can happen when you're alone. Like a crushed piece of grass or a smoldering wick, church appears broken sometimes. But even now, two thousand years after Jesus called people into community, churches still echo the message of Jesus: *You are known. You are loved. You belong.*

1. "Millions of Unchurched Adults Are Christians Hurt by Churches But Can Be Healed of the Pain," Barna, April 12, 2010, https://www.barna.com/research/millions-of-unchurched-adults-are-christians-hurt-by-churches-but-can-be-healed-of-the-pain/.

2. Stephen Mansfield, *Healing Your Church Hurt* (Carol Stream, IL: BarnaBooks, 2010).

CHAPTER 12

Don't Give Up on God

I gave in, and admitted that God was God.
—C. S. Lewis

A recent survey found that 43 percent of millennials (people born between 1984 and 2002) "either don't know, don't care or don't believe God exists."[1] A Gallup poll found a similar pattern across all age groups in the United States: belief in God has hit an all-time low. Interestingly, the poll also revealed that even professed Christians are experiencing growing doubts about God: 39 percent of people who believe in God say that He doesn't hear prayers and/or cannot intervene on our behalf.[2] That's worth pausing and pondering—almost six out of ten *believers* don't *believe* that God hears our prayers or can help us in life. So to summarize the trends: fewer people believe in God, and of those who do, most of them don't believe He can do the things He says He can do.

If you've considered all the suffering in the world or felt overwhelmed by the struggles of the human experience, then you, too, may have wondered if there is a God. And if there is, you may question whether He cares and is involved in your daily life. In the end, is the Bible only folklore and fairy tales? It is, after all, an ancient collection of stories about kings and queens, heroes and villains, espionage and betrayal, curses and cures, monsters and a couple of talking animals.

Even Jesus' friends and followers faced questions about God. Crowds of people had watched Jesus show compassion and perform miracles—they had seen it with their own eyes—but some of them still questioned and complained. The people who had known Him since childhood were especially spiteful, stirring up doubt, saying, "He has some nerve saying He is from *heaven*. We know the grimy town where He was raised—and it is definitely not heaven!"

The skepticism about Jesus grew, and some of the people who had once followed Him abandoned Him. This led Jesus to ask His twelve disciples if they, too, were going to leave. The disciple John described the encounter:

> From this time many of his disciples turned back and no longer followed him.
>
> "You do not want to leave too, do you?" Jesus asked the Twelve.
>
> Simon Peter answered him, "Lord, to whom shall we go? You have the words of eternal life. We have come to believe and to know that you are the Holy One of God" (John 6:66–69).

Surrounded by doubters, questioned by Jesus Himself whether he truly believed, Simon Peter answered simply, "Lord, to whom shall we go?"

You can almost hear the emotion in his voice. "What else is there, Lord? Where else could we go? There is no better way."

I can relate to Simon Peter's declaration. When I consider my options, I could choose to follow a different world religion, or I could abandon the idea of the Unseen Divine altogether. I could explore a path of self-actualization, seeking a god within myself, or I could put my faith in undefined forces and simply "trust the universe."

But when I consider the choices, I, like Simon Peter, lock my eyes on Jesus again and ask, "Where else will I go?" Jesus is the best and truest answer to my questions. I have found no better explanation for the insistent whisper that tells us there is something more. I don't know a better reason for our instinct to worship and our longing for life to be perfect. I haven't heard a worthier explanation for our yearning to be fully known and accepted, our desire to have a purpose and to be part of something bigger than ourselves. I don't know a better reason why we can't seem to let go of the idea that light will conquer darkness.

With Simon Peter, I look honestly at the options, and I fling all my hope on Jesus of Nazareth. As Simon Peter said, "Lord, to whom shall we go? You have the words of eternal life. We have come to believe and to know that you are the Holy One of God" (John 6:68, 69).

When Simon Peter gave that answer, he was face-to-face with Jesus. The Savior was standing in front of him, asking him if he was going to stick with Him and put his hope in Him. For the rest of us, that question comes in much more subtle ways, in quiet moments or in times of doubt. But it comes to us all. Are we going to believe in God and put our hope in Him?

The rest of the prophecy

When Matthew shared the prophecy about the bruised reed and the smoldering wick, he delivered a very important message about the never-give-up God. But interestingly, Matthew didn't quote the entire prophecy. There is a sentence he didn't include that adds even more meaning and hope. To see what is missing, we have to go back to Isaiah 42, where the prophecy was originally recorded. As a reminder, here's part of what Matthew included in his writings:

A bruised reed he will not break,
    and a smoldering wick he will not snuff out,
till he has brought justice through to victory.
    In his name the nations will put their hope (Matthew 12:20, 21).

Matthew shared the section of Isaiah's prophecy that explains that we can trust Jesus not to give up, but Matthew didn't include the part that explains *why* we can trust Jesus. If you look at the original prophecy in Isaiah, you'll see the sentence that Matthew omitted.

Look at what Isaiah wrote, paying close attention to the additional sentence:

> A bruised reed he will not break,
>   and a smoldering wick he will not snuff out.
> In faithfulness he will bring forth justice;
>   *he will not falter or be discouraged*
> till he establishes justice on earth.
>   In his teaching the islands will put their hope
>   (Isaiah 42:3, 4; emphasis added).

This sentence expands the prophecy. It says Jesus "will not falter or be discouraged" (verse 4). In many English translations, as in the one quoted here, the words that are used are *falter* and *be discouraged*. That is beautifully worded, but it loses something significant in translation. In the original Hebrew, the sentence says that Jesus will not "burn dimly" or "be bruised"—the same phrases used earlier to describe the candle that is burning dimly and the reed that is bruised.

So what Isaiah originally wrote sounded more like this:

> A *bruised* reed he will not break,
>   and a *dimly burning* wick he will not snuff out. . . .
> He will not *burn dimly* or *be bruised*.

In other words, in the very areas where you are weak or struggling, Jesus will be strong. When you feel surrounded by darkness and have only a dim light, He will shine brightly for you. When you feel crushed and bruised, He will stand strong on your behalf.

By sharing this prophecy, Matthew was telling us not to give up hope.

In the original prophecy, Isaiah was telling us Jesus *is* the hope.

We don't need to give up hope, because Jesus Himself will be our Hope.

This extra sentence in the prophecy brings a surge of hopefulness into every seemingly hopeless situation because it promises that God will provide what we lack. When we are discouraged, He encourages us. When we don't know what to do, He provides direction. When we feel stuck, He moves us forward. When we don't feel loving, He shows us love.

If you are losing hope in any area of life—people, health, or goals and dreams—it's easy to start feeling like it all depends on you. You feel pressure to formulate a plan, get more motivated, or be more persistent. Those things may help, but this message from Isaiah is a reminder that turning around hopeless situations isn't all on your shoulders. Jesus is the source of hope, and He won't run out of strength, ideas, resources, patience, or love. No matter what, He won't be crushed or burn dimly.

There's enough hope for everyone

Now, this never-give-up prophecy sounds nice, but you might still wonder if it really applies to *you*, right now, in your current circumstances. Isaiah wanted to make sure that everyone who hears this message of hope would know that yes, it is for absolutely everyone. That's why he ended the prophesy with this sentence: "In his teaching the islands will put their hope" (Isaiah 42:4). Matthew paraphrased it this way: "In his name the nations will put their hope" (Matthew 12:21).

The "islands" and "nations"—meaning people from everywhere, including faraway places—will put their hope in Him. Isaiah was reminding us that because Jesus doesn't give up, all of us—everyone, everywhere—can have hope.

That's the amazing thing about hope. It's like God's love—it doesn't run out or have limits. This invitation to hold on to hope wasn't just for people in the days of Isaiah or Matthew. It's for us too—right here, right now. The never-give-up God is still burning brightly and standing strong on behalf of people who put their hope in Him. As A. W. Tozer observed about God: "Anything He did anywhere else He will do here; anything He did any other time He is willing to do now; anything He ever did for other people He is willing to do for us!"[3]

Hope is for all of us.

Get your hopes up

Ultimately, to put your hope in God means to wait with expectation. As I've heard it said, hope is faith in the future tense. It is believing and expecting that God is going to be good to you in the future.

126

Because God hasn't given up, we can trust that He'll breathe new life into even the most hopeless situations. Dimly burning candles can erupt into bright flames. Crushed blades of grass can stretch toward the sky again.

Life will always give you plenty of reasons to lose hope.

But Isaiah reminds us of one really good reason not to lose hope—Jesus is a never-give-up God.

So go ahead. Get your hopes up.

1. "A New Study Says 43 Percent of Millennials Don't Know If, Care or Believe God Exists," *Relevant*, May 17, 2021, https://relevant magazine.com/faith/a-new-study-says-43-percent-of-millennials -dont-know-if-care-or-believe-god-exists/.

2. Jeffrey M. Jones, "Belief in God in U.S. Dips to 81%, a New Low," Gallup, June 17, 2022, https://news.gallup.com /poll/393737/belief-god-dips-new-low.aspx.

3. A. W. Tozer, *When He Is Come: Ten Messages on the Holy Spirit*, ed. and comp. Gerald B. Smith (Harrisburg, PA: Christian Publications, 1968), 123.